MEMORIES OF REVOLUTION

Preserving the childhood memories of some of the last generation of White Russian women to experience the Revolution first-hand, this poignant collection of interviews and photographs provides a unique and moving record of life in Imperial and Bolshevik Russia.

The accounts give a personal insight into how the Revolution devastated the lives of the aristocracy, the intelligentsia and the foreigners of Moscow and St Petersburg in the few weeks after the October 1917 upheaval. These people, previously amongst the wealthiest in Russia, were reduced to a life of poverty, persecution and exile. This forced exile has had a profound effect on these women. Their childhood memories have remained very sharp, with a volume of detail and intensity of recall peculiar to those whose premature transition from child to adult coincided with the traumas of revolution.

Anna Horsbrugh-Porter is a journalist with the BBC World Service. Frances Welch is a freelance journalist who writes on Russian topics for a number of British daily newspapers and journals. Elena Snow is the daughter of two Russian émigrés, and has grown up amongst the White Russian circles in exile in London.

MEMORIES OF REVOLUTION

Russian women remember

Edited by
Anna Horsbrugh-Porter
Interviews by
Elena Snow and Frances Welch

London and New York

First published 1993
by Routledge
11 New Fetter Lane, London EC4P 4EE

Simultaneously published in the USA and Canada
by Routledge
29 West 35th Street, New York, NY 10001

Editorial contribution © 1993 Anna Horsbrugh-Porter

Interviews © 1993 Frances Welch and Elena Snow

Typeset in 10/12pt Palatino by
Ponting–Green Publishing Services,
Chesham, Bucks
Printed and bound in Great Britain by
T. J. Press (Padstow) Ltd, Cornwall

British Library Cataloguing in Publication Data

A catalogue record for this book is available from the British Library

Library of Congress Cataloging in Publication Data

Memories of revolution / [edited by] Anna Horsbrugh-Porter ;
with interviews by Frances Welch and Elena Snow.
p. cm.
Includes bibliographical references and index.
1. Soviet Union–History–Revolution, 1917–1921 – Personal
narratives.   2. Women–Soviet Union–Biography.
I. Horsbrugh-Porter, Anna.   II. Welch, Frances.
III. Snow, Elena.
DK265.69.M46   1993
947.084'1–dc20
92–46113

ISBN 0–415–08806–2 hbk
ISBN 0–415–08807–0 pbk

CONTENTS

ILLUSTRATIONS

ACKNOWLEDGEMENTS

We wish to thank all those who were willing to be interviewed for this book and for lending their photographs – Anya Troup, Tatiana Vladimirovna Toporkova, Princess Sophia Wacznadze, Dorothy Russell, Irina Sergevna Tidmarsh, Ludmila Mathias, Marie Allan, Olga Lawrence, Eugenia Peacock, Ada Nikolskaya.

RUSSIAN EMPIRE CIRCA 1900

Franz-Josef Land

GERMAN EMPIRE

SWEDEN

NORWAY

ARCT

Berlin

Gulf of Bothnia

BARENTS-SEA

Vienna

BALTIC SEA

Murmansk

Novaia Zemlia

AUSTRIA-HUNGARY

Budapest

Warsaw

Revel

Finland

Helsingfors (Helsinki)

KARA SEA

SERBIA

Poland

Riga

WHITE SEA

Sofia

BULGARIA

Brest-Litovsk

Vilno

Pskov

St. Petersburg (Petrograd)

Archangel

Arctic Circle

ROMANIA

Bucharest

Minsk

Novgorod

Smolensk

Kiev

Odessa

OTTOMAN EMPIRE

Constantinople (Istanbul)

Gallipoli

Dnieper

Poltava

Briansk

Moscow

Vologda

Northern Dvina

Ob

Mountains

Sevastopol

Crimea

BLACK SEA

SEA OF AZOV

Kharkov

Lipetsk

Riazan

Nizhnii Novgorod

Penza

Volga

Kazan

Perm

Ekaterinburg (Sverdlovsk)

Ural

West

Donetsk

RUSSIA

Don

Saratov

Tsaritsyn (Volgograd)

Simbirsk

Samara

Ufa

Tobolsk

Stavropol

Ural

Orenburg

Siberia

Irtysh

Ob

Caucasus Mts.

Astrakhan

Orsk

Ishim

Tiflis (Tblisi)

Erivan

CASPIAN SEA

Baku

Transiberian Railroad

Omsk

Tomsk

Baghdad

Novonikolaevsk (Novosibirsk)

Tehran

ARAL SEA

Turkestan

Lake Balkash

Barnaul

Semipalatinsk

PERSIA

Askhabad

Amu Daria

Bukhara

Syr Daria

Tashkent

Vernyi

Ili

Samarkand

Fergana

AFGHANISTAN

Kabul

BRITISH INDIA

0   200   400   600   800   1000 Miles

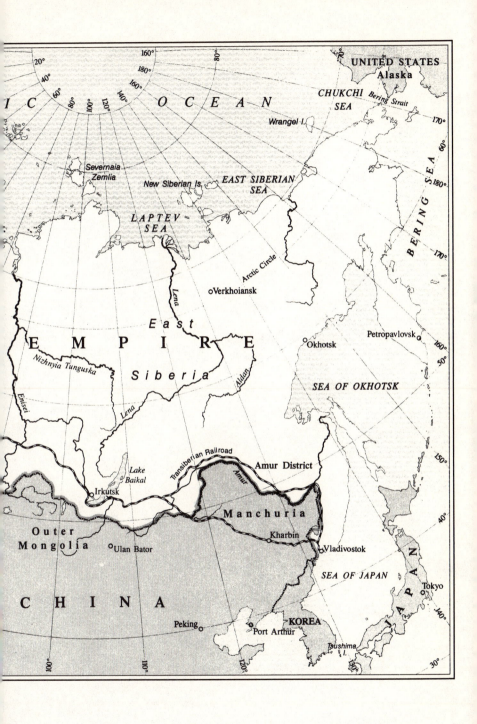

INTRODUCTION

Over two million Russians went into exile after 1917 to escape persecution under Bolshevik rule. This book is about just ten of these emigrés, a tiny proportion of the huge diaspora of Russians who settled all over the world. The 1917 wave of refugees was formed from a very specialised section of pre-revolutionary Russia. They were an alliance of anti-Bolshevik elements; they came from the nobility and privileged classes, the educated intelligentsia, merchants, industrialists, those who had foreign connections or were political opponents of the new regime like the Socialist Revolutionaries, Mensheviks and Kadets. Collectively, they are known as 'White Russians' because of their support for the White army during the 1918–20 Russian civil war, a force composed of the same anti-Bolshevik elements as the refugees themselves. (The White Russians of 1917 are not to be confused with the inhabitants of Belarus – meaning white Russia – the old republic of Byelorussia, and now member of the Commonwealth of Independent States.)

This book tells the stories of ten women, all from the privileged classes, who lived through the time of revolution and its after effects. A collection of oral histories such as this always presents problems. How can the written word ever convey the intimacy and emotional effect of actually hearing someone recount their life history? In particular, how can it represent the authentic voices of these women, all in their eighties and nineties, often sitting in rooms filled with relics from their Russian childhoods? Although most have lived only a fraction of their lives in Russia, all speak in heavily accented, idiomatic English, which again cannot be transposed to the printed page. But oral history at its best is a vivid insight into a life, a unique source of information which lets us see external events filtered through individual experience. In the past,

1

it has often given a voice to those who go unrecorded, who don't write biographies. For this reason, oral historians have usually focused on the underprivileged, recording their experience of privation and disadvantage, to set against the 'official' recorded histories. *Memories of Revolution* breaks with tradition in this respect. Its subjects are members of the most privileged, articulate, educated and active part of pre-revolutionary Russian society.

These are ten women of the last generation who witnessed the 1917 Revolution at first hand, who remember what Russia was like at the beginning of the century, and what it meant to belong to the nobility and intelligentsia at that time. Their experiences are not part of official Soviet history, yet the Russian Revolution was perhaps the single most important event of this century, and for that reason these eye-witness accounts deserve to be recorded.

The subjects are all women, partly just because the majority of the first generation White Russian community in exile were women. This can be ascribed to female longevity, and the fact that more daughters than sons escaped with their parents after 1917. Sons, if old enough, would have fought and perhaps died in the White Russian army, as Irina Tidmarsh's brother Rafa did. There was also the Bolshevik disregard of female children as Olga Lawrence mentions in her story. She and her two sisters were eventually allowed to leave after a year of wrangling with the authorities. Their success was due to the Bolsheviks' 'useless mouths' theory. Daughters of the intelligentsia and aristocracy were not wanted in the new Soviet state, because they were perceived as useless. It was Russian men the Bolsheviks needed, among them Olga Lawrence's male cousins, who couldn't escape and later died.

We also chose to interview only women, not so much to draw gender-specific conclusions from their experiences, but to see what they thought as young girls who were not expected to fight, or take an active part in the Revolution. Their reactions to 1917 concentrate on how their lives were changed. To them, the Revolution spelt material deprivation and emotional trauma, the loss of fathers, uncles, brothers. Invariably their mothers, sisters and aunts took over as head of the family. Both mothers and daughters had to work for the first time. Fathers were mostly absent, in prison or exile. The confusion followed immediately after the Bolshevik takeover of November 1917 (NS). These children of wealthy merchants, politicians and intelligentsia were suddenly thrown into a state of near starvation and subjected to regular house searches, where death was the penalty if the soldiers found any money, jewellery, weapons or evidence of anti-Bolshevik connections. They had been used to the privileged life of dachas, servants, an abundance of rich food, a succession of foreign governesses and tutors and houses in Moscow and St Petersburg – a life Irina Tidmarsh records in her story. Now, often in the space of a few weeks, all their possessions were appropriated or stolen, flats and houses were requisitioned, servants fled and the family disintegrated.

All these women have survived horrifying events, both personal and political. But to a great extent they have remained Russian, and are still firmly attached to the values of the class and status they were born into. Most of them married Europeans, and have lived a life consistent with their pre-revolutionary experiences. They talk affectionately of Tsarist Russia, and see the immediate pre-revolutionary period as a hierarchical Utopia which was destroyed by the Bolsheviks. In fact, historians have described this last generation of White Russians as living on a fault line – on the brink of disintegration since the student disturbances in Russian universities of the late 1890s. The Russian aristocracy and intelligentsia of the 1900s inherited a doomed and degenerating system. And at the end of the twentieth century – when the old Soviet empire has collapsed, and Soviet communism has been relegated to history – the fate of Russia and the other former Soviet republics again hangs in the balance, as it did in 1917.

The historical framework of the book is the events surrounding the Russian Revolution of 1917, when the violent overthrow and murder of the Tsar ended 1,000 years of princely and Tsarist rule in the Russian lands. Twelve years earlier, the first Russian Revolution of 1905 established the basis for what followed. Its underlying causes were social discontent, the recent humiliation of the Russian defeat in the Russo/Japanese war (1904–5), strikes and demonstrations. Its actual catalyst was the massacre of peaceful demonstrators on 22 January (9 January OS) outside the Tsar's Winter Palace in St Petersburg – afterwards called Bloody Sunday. The uprising which followed forced Nicholas II's hand, and he made an unwilling gesture towards constitutional monarchy by establishing a Duma – supposedly an elected reformist parliament. The Duma's effectiveness was constrained by the

3

Tsar's powers to dissolve it, and it was swept away in 1917 by revolution. In January 1917, the food supply to St Petersburg had broken down, and it was women who were the first to riot over the shortages as Irina Tidmarsh remembers. The worsening situation at the war front, where the badly equipped, badly led Russian army was suffering huge defeats on all sides, also fuelled frustration. On 15 March 1917 Tsar Nicholas II was forced to abdicate, and the Romanov dynasty – which had ruled for over 300 years – ended. A Provisional Government was appointed and the eight months that followed were a strange lull in Russia's history. Irina Tidmarsh remembers that period as one of intense public discussion. She says there seemed to be a public meeting on every corner, where Muscovites debated Russia's future. While they talked, they chewed sunflower seeds, and she remembers vividly piles of seed husks all over the streets, as a relic of the men and women who'd met, talked, eaten – and then left, as the Bolsheviks ended all discussion with their coup d'état on 8 November 1917. They took over St Petersburg in a virtually bloodless coup; in Moscow there was fighting for about a week, with small pockets of resistance also flaring up in other parts of the country. But in St Petersburg, the Bolsheviks formed a new government led by Lenin, and broke for good with the Mensheviks. It's at this point that most of the women's memories of revolution begin – from the moment the Provisional Government was brought down and the Russian Communist Party, as the Bolsheviks rechristened themselves, began the radical reforms that determined the course of twentieth-century history.

They swiftly abolished private property – so all the dachas, farms and country estates of the privileged classes were immediately requisitioned. Inherited wealth was abolished, as were legal class privileges and titles. The calendar was reformed to bring Russia in line with the rest of Western Europe. Previously Russia had followed the Julian calendar, thirteen days behind the Gregorian, which Western Europe used; this is why there are two dates, pre- and post-revolutionary for the same event, referred to as Old and New Style (OS/NS).

The White army organised its resistance, and as the months went on the Bolsheviks responded with persecution and suppression of perceived anti-Bolshevik elements. They insisted on one-party Bolshevik rule, and set up the first secret police, the Cheka, an acronym for the 'All Russian Extraordinary Commission for

Combating Counter-revolution and Sabotage'. This brutal system, established in December 1917, was the forerunner of the KGB, headed by the notorious Felix Dzerzhinski. Marie Allan described her meeting with Dzerzhinski, when she had to plead with him for her father's release from prison. At first the White counter-revolution had some success: they gained control of the area around the Volga river to the Pacific ocean, and a stronghold in the Crimea – which is where Sophia Wacznadze's family made for safety. But the resources of the White army were gradually depleted, their offensives failed, and by 1920 they posed no serious threat at all. The Bolsheviks intensified their campaign of wiping out the opposition – real or imagined. Thousands were imprisoned or murdered – like many of the women's fathers. This was also the great period of Russian emigration, as people took to the roads to escape, north through Scandinavia and then to Britain, south through Soviet Central Asia, and on to China and Turkey.

It is against this background of political revolution and brutal persecution that the experience of exile has a particular significance. Forced exile for political reasons, and at such a young age, has had a profound effect on all the contributors. Their childhood memories have remained very sharp, with a volume of detail and intensity of recall that is probably unique to those whose premature transition from child to adult coincided with bloody revolution. But involuntary and unexpected exile has caused all these women to re-create their childhoods as idylls. What follows is a confusing tragedy. Many of these women want to return to die in Russia, and it seems for some as if nothing else in their lives matched their early experiences. They often say how, when they first came out, many of them believed exile would only be a matter of months or a year at most. As a result, they escaped taking very little money and few possessions with them, expecting to return once the Bolsheviks had been overthrown and order restored. In the following years, they had to accept that their lives in Russia had ended; then their childhood memories crystallised, and took on added clarity and significance, due in part to the shock that ended them.

The value of oral history is in its unique quality of personal experience, not historical accuracy. Historical events often become distorted, or marginalised. What emerges is a totally individual and vulnerable world, centred on a child's imagination and interpretation of events as they affect her. Some experiences are shared – in particular the external quality of life peculiar to the Russian intelligentsia, with its routines of comfort, cushions of wealth and numerous domestic servants. There's a strong emphasis on female education which emerges in all the stories. Most pre-revolutionary households had foreign governesses for the children, who in turn were encouraged, if not forced, to become polyglots early on. Many of the women describe their family practice of having set days for different languages. For instance, English would be spoken on Mondays and Tuesdays, French on Wednesdays and Thursdays, with Friday and Saturday reserved for German, and Russian officially spoken only on Sundays. Many continued to study for their school entrance exams right through the Revolution if they possibly could. Tatiana Toporkova's story is centred on the famous Ekaterinensky Institute in St Petersburg, and stands as a unique record of this élite boarding school. Irina Tidmarsh describes with relish her liberating – if shortlived – experience during the Provisional Government, when pupils took over the running of the schools themselves.

Each woman's experience is unique, yet they come from a shared social and cultural background, and might coincide with the others in areas they had in common, such as education, or the pre-revolutionary privileges enjoyed by a certain class. If the formative experience in Tatiana Toporkova's life was attending the Institute, then for Marie Allan it was her father's imprisonment and her subsequent attempts – while impersonating her mother – to plead for his release with Dzerzhinski. Eugenia Peacock can remember in great detail her peripatetic life in Soviet Central Asia in the 1920s and 1930s and Sophia Wacznadze's most vivid memory is of her surreal and fantastic adventure crossing the Black Sea into Turkish exile, lost in the fog and running out of fuel. Certain objects are common to practically all the stories. One is the rough *teplushki* – or goods van used for transporting cattle by rail – which carried many of the women into exile.

The strength of the histories is their visual description and their immediacy; the intensity of the memory is often conveyed by the present tense. Some of the women met famous people of the period, and their impressions as a child have remained with them – Ludmila Mathias' critical memories of Mayakovsky and Gorky, Anya Troup's of her godfather Leo Tolstoy, and Irina Tidmarsh's extraordinary circle of family and friends living in their dacha

6

outside Moscow. After the Revolution, many of the women's strongest memories are of the scarcity of food, and the struggle to survive, buying and selling on the black market. But it's significant that no one dies of starvation. This was the class that still had possessions to sell on the black market. For all their deprivations, they were still not among those who starved in the harsh winter immediately following the 1917 Revolution.

Ludmila Mathias stands apart from the other nine women. She was not a 'White Russian', nor was she persecuted by the Bolsheviks, nor forced into exile, although once Stalin came to power it was impossible for her family to return. Her father was a Bolshevik – Leonid Krassin – who was Commissar for Foreign Trade under Lenin, and held various posts abroad after the Revolution. She is included because her family came from the same class as the other women, and lived in a similar way. Following 1917, the Krassin family was treated with a mixture of curiosity and distaste in Europe, in contrast to the White Russian refugees, who were generally received with open arms. Ada Nikolskaya is the only one of the ten not to have left Russia after 1917, although her family faced the same dangers as the others, due to their élitist connections. Her father was imprisoned, tortured and finally murdered by the Bolsheviks, and she lived with her family through the ravages of Stalin's repressions.

The stories are arranged chronologically according to when the women left Russia, starting with Anya Troup who left before the 1917 Revolution, and ending with Ada Nikolskaya who still lives in Moscow. There's another chronological framework to this book, two events which are described by the women. The experience of revolution, of dramatic upheaval and mass suffering is enclosed by two separate tragedies. In May 1896, nearly 1,400 people are thought to have been crushed to death on Khodynka field, waiting to be given presents by Tsar Nicholas II on his coronation. It was considered a bad omen for his reign. And on 9 March 1953 – as Ada Nikolskaya describes – so many people were crushed to death in the crowds forced to attend Josef Stalin's funeral that Moscow ran out of coffins that day.

Anna Horsbrugh-Porter
1993

ANYA TROUP

Anya Troup was abandoned by her father, and brought up by a female member of Tolstoy's circle in Moscow. They left Russia after the first Revolution in 1905 and came to Britain. She married and has one surviving daughter. Anya Troup died in 1989 – she was 99 years old.

I was born in a village outside Moscow. I'm 98; I was born on 28 October 1890. I've got it written down in my passport, but that's upstairs. I don't think my mother was anybody in particular. . . . She was just in the dacha,[1] outside Moscow; she died in childbirth.

My father was in the army, and he had no use for me at all. I don't even remember the name; I don't think I ever saw him. Oh yes, I did, yes he had the dacha in the village where my grandmother lived and where she looked after me first. He used to have it always locked up; my grandmother wasn't allowed to use it or anything, or only when he had leave and some of his officers came back. Then some of his dacha was opened out, and they came and enjoyed their leave. And I remember my grandmother taking me over to him when he had arrived with some of his soldiers, and they were all drunk I suppose. Anyway they put me on a table, I remember this quite well, and told me to dance. So there was small me jigging about on a table in my father's dacha which was opened out when he came back. I thought he was dreadful making me dance in front of all the drunk soldiers.

My grandmother used to look after me and then she got a bit elderly and couldn't cope, so she said to my father, 'What do I do with the child?' and he said, 'Oh well, we'd better get her adopted.' She thought that was a good idea, and thought she ought to choose somebody nice to get me adopted. He himself was in the army, and he couldn't really be bothered very much; you know he was always in some skirmish or whatever, and was

8

finally killed in the Russian–Japanese war.[2] Anyway, so then I think my grandmother had a friend who knew the Tolstoy family, and said did they know anybody who wanted to adopt a little girl, a baby girl? They said they'd look around, and they looked around, and then I think this is where Tolstoy came in. He said, 'Oh yes, there are lots of people who would like to adopt her I'm sure,' and so he found my adopted mother. She was an artist, in the Western Art School in Moscow, and her friend, an English lady, who was called Mary Shanks – the daughter of a wealthy English merchant in Moscow.

My adopted mother had a very sad life; all her family was consumptive, all her sisters and relations had died of consumption so she was delicate and so on, and had a miserable existence really. I don't know how she got to know Tolstoy, but anyway she did, and it was only when she got to know the Shanks that she came to herself a bit, and went to the art school, and then life was a bit easier for her. She thought, and everybody around her thought, that it would be a very good idea if she did adopt a small girl to take her mind off all the difficulties she'd been through. So that's how she came to have me. She lived in a flat belonging to the Shanks's house, which was big, and I was 5 when I was adopted. It was all done through lawyers and that sort of thing, and Tolstoy became my guardian.

I remember sitting by the window for a long time once I'd got there, waiting for my grandmother to come back and fetch me. And she didn't come, and I wouldn't eat anything, and so they said, 'Well you'd better come to bed.' My adopted mother had made, or bought, a very attractive pair of bedroom slippers, and I took a great fancy to these bedroom slippers and I condescended to go to bed in the bedroom slippers, just as long as I could wear them.

Did you ever see your grandmother again?

No . . . no . . . no, certainly not, never, it was all done by lawyers, and so on, and everything was cut and dried. I called Tolstoy my godfather because he made himself responsible for me, because he'd found me, and engineered the whole thing. I remember Tolstoy very well; he had a white horse he always used to ride on the estate.[3] I was lifted by him onto his white horse; I was very thrilled, but I was a bit nervous, because for a child being on a horse is always rather alarming. And then those clothes he always

9

wore, always as a peasant, he had to be a peasant and so on. But, I used to laugh at some of his friends because the peasant garments they wore were always made of the best silk and the best wool. I didn't really know his wife, except that I didn't think much of her. She was fat, and didn't seem to have much use for children. But we used to go and stay there, because my mother didn't like Moscow, and when she wasn't at the art school we used to go down and stay with them, and they had a dacha, which was used for friends, and which was always occupied by various Tolstoyians.

When Tolstoy was out of favour,[4] then everything, all his manuscripts and so on, they were all forbidden. So then my mother started a circle, a Tolstoyian circle, which we had in this flat in the Shanks's house. She used to gather all of his followers, and read out his manuscripts which were all forbidden at that time. But then the police got wise that she was having meetings of these Tolstoyians, which was not allowed because he in those days was taboo. Once the police had discovered this of course my mother was arrested, and given a week to leave. Mary Shanks was English, and so she said, 'I'll come with you,' because she had got an English passport, and she thought that would probably help us, which it did . . . well we think it did. And so, we left with just nothing, just our belongings, and the other person that travelled with us was Pasternak,[5] who was the wife of the painter, and she had two small boys. They were in the same circle as my mother.

The Pasternak woman had a newborn baby, practically newborn, because she wanted to smuggle it out of Russia, so she wouldn't have to register it as a Russian citizen – once you're a Russian citizen you've had it. And she wanted it to be registered in England, so she came out with us. Well, we travelled as I say with this poor woman and she had a hell of a time, with this tiny baby wrapped up in one of those travelling rugs that one had in the old days, like carpets. The two boys and myself were all about the same age, and we thought it would be very funny if the baby screamed just as the train inspectors came around, or gendarmes, or whatever. However, that didn't happen. The baby wasn't discovered, so all was well.

On the journey, my mother always used to say, 'Now soon we'll see the sea, marvellous, I haven't seen the sea for years.' and I thought it was going to be something wonderful, and when I finally did see it, I thought it was terribly uninteresting. To this

day I don't like the sea, but that was just by the way. I remember
my great excitement on the station when we arrived. I think it was
Mary Shanks' sister Louise who met us. She was married to
Aylmer Maude, who was the first translator of Tolstoy's works
into English. And they lived in England, near Chelmsford in
Essex; I think it's called Baddow. And so we parked ourselves on
them, in Little Baddow, and they had built their own dacha, in the
Russian style. The Maudes' house looked like a Russian dacha,
and she used to try and dress herself rather like the Russians, very
tied up in a frock and boots although she was English. I think she
was really more entitled to the honour of being Russian than the
others because I think she knew more Russian than Mary Shanks
or Aylmer Maude for that matter, because they were both English
you see. But Louise Shanks was born in Russia and knew Russian
properly, so I think the honour really was more on her.

There were four Maude sons, and they were the plague of my
life, because I was younger than any of them, and they were
always teasing me, and I always remember them trying to teach
me to ride a bicycle; they put me on a bike, steadied me off and
then let me go, so of course I fell down. And so they kept us, as
refugees more or less, with no money; the Old Man Shanks cut off
the last of his daughters who came with us, because he was so
angry that she came away with my mother. There was also
Chertkov,[6] who was a very great friend of Tolstoy's. He was
thrown out of Russia, but he was high-up aristocracy, and they
couldn't ban him, so they merely asked him to remove himself out
of Russia. He was banned because he was a Tolstoyian, and he
came to England also, and he bought a house in Christchurch I
think it was, and built a small printing factory where forbidden
manuscripts that had been sent out in letter form were published.
People like me, and various other friends, used to post letters to
him, and he had them printed at this printing place, and then I
suppose that Aylmer Maude helped with it; I don't know how the
business went on. Anyway, that was always rather exciting; we
used to go down and stay with him, and he used to send some of
those manuscripts back to us at the Maudes, or back to my
mother, so that all her friends that used to gather could read them.

After two years we bought a little house when the money came
through, near Chelmsford itself, just a little one, because there
were quite a few Russians who were coming over from Russia,
escaping like we did, and they used to come to us. It was

11

somewhere where they knew they could go. But then, after about two or three years I suppose, we moved to Devon. Old Man Shanks used to come over every year with his business, and he always used to take a daughter with him, because he had these five daughters. And once he had taken Mary to Devon when he came over, and she fell in love with Devon; she thought it was a gorgeous place. We went to Teignmouth and had a very nice little Georgian house there, up on the hill, looking over to the sea and the rocks, so that was my home really, until I got married.

In Devon, one of Tolstoy's daughters came to stay with us. She had run away from her husband, with her two children, small boys, and well she just went off, and I think he was probably rather unpleasant; I don't remember all their complications. She didn't live with us for very long, but I think she escaped to us; we were the only people I suppose she knew in England.

I have a lot of Russian things, that came to me in rather a funny way, I think about three or four years after we did. Whole crates of stuff came over. Who got them packed up and sent over I haven't a clue; I suppose one of the Shanks. What my mother was looking forward to was a lovely fur coat, and she said she'd never been cold until she came to England, and she was looking forward to this fur coat which never came.

In the 1917 Revolution in Russia, all the banks announced that if anybody had any valuables, they ought to give them up.[7] So I think a lot of the English, and I suppose other countries, rushed madly to Russia to see what they could salvage from this announcement. And there's a Russian jeweller's shop in London, in Regent Street, and he had quite a lot of stuff – Fabergé's things and so on. There were also these earrings, straight from the Revolution. Yes, these belonged to Catherine the Great of Russia, and were given to her by one of her lovers, of whom she had many, to lock up the secrets that were whispered in her ears. So one's a lock, and one's a key. I wore them soon after that Revolution, when the stuff came over; I don't know, 1918 I think. And I sleep in them, have my hair washed in them; I never take them off, I always think it's dangerous to start taking them off.

1 Anya Troup with her daughter

2 Anya Troup in 1988, aged 98

3 Tolstoy at Yasnaya Polyana – a painting owned by Anya Troup

4 Tatiana Toporkova (centre) with her brother, sister and governess at Peterhof

5 Tatiana Toporkova aged 7, with her father and brother in Finland (1908)

6 Tatiana Toporkova aged 12, wearing the uniform of the
St Catherine Institute in St Petersburg

7 Princess Sophia Wacznadze (child on right)

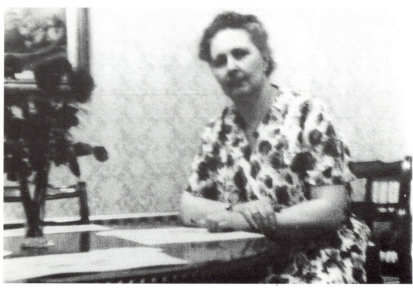

8 Princess Sophia Wacznadze

9 Dorothy Russell (centre) with a miniature samovar and tea set

10 Irina Tidmarsh in
1914 at Belokolodez

11 Belokolodez

12 Irina
Tidmarsh with
her brother Rafa
in 1915

13 Irina Tidmarsh in 1919

14 (From left to right) Ludmila Mathias with her sisters
Louba and Katia at Tsarskoe Selo in 1917

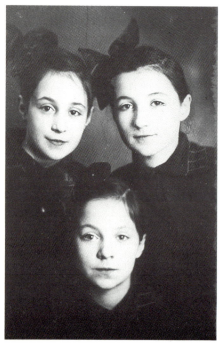

15 Ludmila Mathias
(right) with her
sisters Katia (left)
and Louba (below)

16 Marie Allan (front right) with her family in Moscow, 1907

17 Marie Allan aged 14,
in Moscow

18 Marie Allen aged 13 in 1915, in Moscow

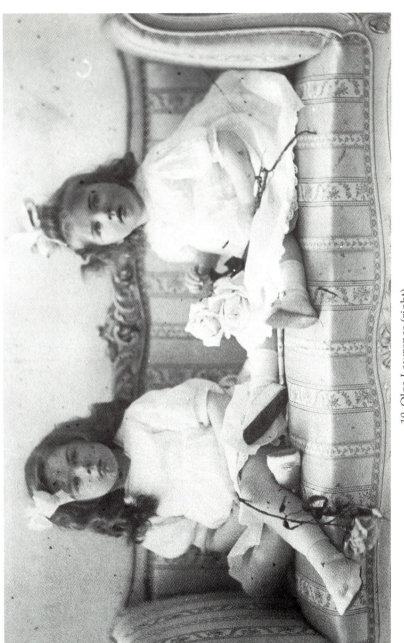

19 Olga Lawrence (right)

21 Eugenia Peacock at Diadino in 1917/18

20 Eugenia Peacock at Talozhnya in 1915

23 Eugenia Peacock

22 Eugenia Peacock

24 Ada Nikolskaya in
May 1990

25 Tatiana Toporkova, Irina Tidmarsh and Eugenia Peacock

TATIANA VLADIMIROVNA
TOPORKOVA

Tatiana Vladimirovna Toporkova was born in St Petersburg in 1901. Her father was in the Imperial Russian Baltic Navy, and was often sent on missions abroad. In 1910, the family of two daughters and two sons joined their father at the embassy in London, but Tatiana went back to be educated in Russia. With the 1917 Bolshevik Revolution, the embassy was disbanded, and the family moved. In 1920, Tatiana married her husband – a revolutionary. They lived around the world, and had one son. For twenty years she worked at the Monitoring Service of the BBC, and then for the UN in Geneva. She now lives in Reading.

I was born in St Petersburg, when it was still St Petersburg and subsequently became Leningrad of course. And that was in 1901. It was in the Nadezhdinskaya Street, which gave on to the Liteiny Prospekt, which was a very busy thoroughfare leading into the Nevsky.[1] Of course I don't remember it; my parents must have moved quite soon afterwards. My father was in the services. He was basically a naval officer in the Baltic fleet. But he was also a member of the *Gvardeisky Ekipazh* (Guards Corps) and I always ascribe to this why he was constantly sent on various assignments and missions, not only serving in the fleet. He had been trained as a mechanical engineer and that was quite a new discipline in those days because the fleet had only just been transferred to steam. My grandfather was also in the navy, and he was an admiral; he was still commanding windjammers. Steamships were brought in somewhere in the middle of the nineteenth century,[2] so that young boys who had a training in engineering were very valuable. My father used to say the best thing his own father had done for him was to persuade him to take up engineering. Grandfather knew or felt that all this travelling under sail would stop and that everything would be transferred to steam.

13

My first recollection is when we lived in Vindava, now called Ventspils in Latvia; it was on the Baltic coast, because my father was supervising the construction of a ship. I remember playing in the sand dunes there. I had a brother and a sister and I was the youngest and there we had a German governess called Fräulein Erica. I remember the house where we lived and I also remember being locked up in a little box room we had, which was between the kitchen and my parents' bedroom. And when I had been particularly naughty, I was locked up there. I didn't mind at all; I'd just sit there, and from time to time my father would come up and say something like 'Now, are you going to behave yourself?' and I'd say 'No'. He'd say 'Nu sidi' (Then stay), and then again another thing he used to say 'Ty budesh tsarapatsya?' (Will you scratch your brother's face?). And I used to shout 'Budu, budu, budu, budu' (I will, I will, I will, I will). And so on. And in the end, when I got really tired, next time he came round and said something like 'Now, are you going to behave yourself?' I'd say 'Yes, I want to get out of here and I'll never do it again, and I'm so sorry' and I cried, and he let me out.

When my father was away for several years in the Far East, during the Japanese campaign of 1904, we three children, our German nursery-governess and an old nurse lived in a small flat in St Petersburg. We lived in this flat because we were still too young to go to school, any of us, even my eldest sister. I think they'd just started preparing her for her entrance exam for the Institute.[3] She was nearly five years older than me, so she must have been 8. Now most schools in Russia at that time started at 10 and before that we had a governess. I still remember going with my mother to the kitchen to take part in the letter-writing ceremony. Our old nurse was completely illiterate and other neighbouring servants came with their own requests. We had only oil lamps in the flat and I remember one with a green shade lighting the table at which my mother was sitting, while several women stood in the shadows and dictated in a monotonous voice. It seemed to me that all they did was send endless greetings to all the members of the village commune, each of whom had to be mentioned fully with name and patronymic. I asked my mother why such a dull letter had to be sent, and she explained that it was most important not to forget anyone, otherwise an ignored villager would be terribly hurt and feel insulted.

My father was absent then for about three years, because he was in the Far East, and he was one of the few survivors of the Japanese war.[4] The whole of that fleet perished and it was quite by chance that he wasn't there at the time and survived. Then he was interned in Sarawak (Borneo) and Sumatra, in Indonesia, until it was all over, until the peace treaty had been signed, and then he returned back. It was a great excitement because I hardly remembered him except for those incidents when I was locked up. Of course my mother was always writing to him, and sending postcards and my sister signed them because I didn't write yet. So there was always a contact and we knew there was a father there. There was great excitement when he came back. He'd completely changed; he'd lost all his hair and he was bald, whereas as a young man he was terribly hairy, you know hirsute, with an awful lot of wavy hair and a beard.

What was your parents' relationship like?

As children we really couldn't judge how our parents got on together, and it was a period when I was in the hands of a governess and preparing to go to school. My sister had gone to school already and my brother was being coached for entrance exams. So we didn't have all that much to do with our parents and then my little brother arrived soon after that, Dima. He is much younger than us, and he was brought up completely separately.

My father was sent to Finland, and he took us all with him. He was supervising some new boat-building for the reconstruction of the fleet; they had to replenish the whole fleet as they had lost nearly all the ships. The Zavod Kreitona In Turku in Finland was building for the Russian navy, and it's very amusing that I found through listening to Moscow radio that this shipyard still exists. It is still working for the Russian government. So the contact must have gone on for sixty or seventy years.

I was too young for school; my sister was already sent to school at that time, to the Institute. It was the Ekaterinensky Institute, on the Fontanka[5] in St Petersburg, again very central, not far from where I was born. You started there at the age of 10, and you had to pass a little entrance exam to start at the school proper; it was only for girls. In a way it was a bit like an 11-plus.

We stayed in Finland for a year, and then we returned to Petersburg and we lived there for a couple of years. My father was sent to Central Asia I remember, on a big mission, when the Khan of Khiva and Emir of Bokhara were still independent,[6] and they had to swear loyalty to the Russian crown. So a mission was sent out to Bokhara, and my father was in that mission. That only happened in my lifetime; before that they were completely independent. Just as people don't realise how independent Georgia was,[7] you only know it really from reading Lermontov.[8] All these troops were sent there, and there were still quite a number of tribes like the Chechens, Ingush and others and these wild men in the mountains were really very anti-Russian. I'm sure there are still some living up in the mountains you know, who go from generation to generation not really taking in what is really happening, or who is really governing them. So I remember my father going off on that mission, and he brought back a couple of rugs and a sword, a marvellous sword, all covered in jewels. I think we left that in Russia as far as I remember; it was too cumbersome to carry and anyway we always thought we were going to return. Then he was appointed to the embassy in London. He was sent again on a special mission working for the Admiralty; his job was mainly to buy the coal for the navy because by that time it was all steamships. I remember he was always going to Wales or up to Newcastle; I suppose that kind of anthracite they hadn't got in Russia at all, or they weren't mining it.

As soon as we heard that he was going to be appointed to London our governess changed immediately. My mother went and engaged an English governess. She was Nelly Callender, a real Scots girl, who spoke with a strong Scottish accent and so we rolled our 'r's and shortened our vowels in English. I must have been already then about 7 or 8. We weren't terribly fond of her and I'm afraid we weren't very nice to her. She was only about 18 or 20, quite a young girl. My mother always preferred young governesses because she said they play with the children, they're much better than having somebody older. She just couldn't cope very well poor girl, now when I think about it. In the beginning we still went to Peterhof[9] for the summers, where my father was originally engaged on the royal yacht. I remember going out with my father at Peterhof to the parks. He would start off by tipping the attendants of the various tricks and follies; the park was full of these eighteenth-century tricks. You rang a bell and all the ducks came out and then there was a big mushroom – you had to stand under the mushroom, and it rained as soon as you got under it.

In September 1910 we left to join father in London, who had already taken up his post here. Arriving was very exciting; first of all travelling on a boat direct from Petersburg to London. We had some bad weather in the North Sea, terribly exciting, people were sick. We were good sailors fortunately so that was all right. We arrived somewhere in the port of London in one of the docks where my father met us and I remember a little taxi which then drove through London to Richmond, to Richmond Terrace, looking over the Thames.

The very next morning after our arrival, my father took me to a local private school in Richmond. And I thought that was unfair because, well we were still very unsettled, it wasn't our home, we hadn't the usual governess. For the first few weeks or so I was pretty lost. They were all very interested, because after all a Russian girl they'd never seen. I didn't terribly like it there; well I suppose it was a bit traumatic for a child of 9 to suddenly find oneself in completely different surroundings. I'd never even been to school in Russia.

During the First World War I stayed on in London and we had a marvellous Russian teacher who turned out to be a terrible revolutionary. He disappeared in 1917 and he was teaching all the embassy children. He was called Leonid Pokrovsky; he was a very unprepossessing ugly little man who was obviously an emigré. This teacher Pokrovsky actually coached my brother for entering the naval academy in Petersburg and he also gave lessons in Russian and Russian literature to me, and he was also teaching the Volkov children who were the other embassy family. So as I say, this rabid revolutionary was teaching all the government children.

In the meantime, applications and registrations were started for my taking up a place at the Institute in St Petersburg and in less than two years of my permanent stay in England, I started my yearly journeys to boarding school in Russia. In the autumn of 1912 when they took my sister back after the summer holidays, I had to go as well. But our summer holidays we continued in the Russian way in Britain; my parents would take a furnished house which was our 'dacha'. One year we went to Wales, another year we were in Devonshire and then my father wanted to be nearer to London, and so we were in Surrey. The dacha was a rented house, like it was done in Russia, and we had endless visitors. In the beginning of course, we had a lot of visitors from Russia, up till the 1914 war.

When I returned to Russia, for the Institute, I hadn't been out for so long, only two or three years. My mother was with us; by that time she started travelling backwards and forwards, and knew her way about as she said. So sometimes we crossed through Holland and sometimes the direction was Germany, and we stopped in Berlin. And those lovely Russian trains! They were so big and comfortable and we had so much room, and always the samovar[10] in the corridor. We always stopped at my uncle's in Petersburg; well, my mother wasn't going to book rooms at hotels, it wasn't done in those days. So we always landed on my uncle, and we had about a week there and we enjoyed ourselves. My mother used to take us out and buy things for us and go and visit our old friends and we had other contacts there, and only then were we taken to school.

We had a very strict uniform; we still wore the old eighteenth-century uniform with long dresses down to our ankles, and pinafores that went over them and that were laced at the back. The dress was laced at the back as well, and it was an awful nuisance, because if you were late and couldn't get up in the morning, you couldn't just slip on your dress and be there as the bell went, you still had to be laced in. So there was this long dress that was very tight, and there was a little short cape and also some white longish sleeves, not a cuff, but it came over your dress sleeves – it was supposed to keep the sleeves clean. If we were ever caught – 'Oh it's dirty, take it off!' – we had to put clean ones on. It was a very practical idea, because they could be changed more often.

I remember going to the Institute, and having to take this little exam and then I was curtseying hard to everybody, including the priest who came in; it was a terrible *faux pas*. There he was the only person you had to bow to. Everybody else you had to curtsey to. The first Institute was created by Catherine,[11] on the lines of St Cyr in France, because St Cyr used to be a girls' school. By the beginning of the nineteenth century, Catherine's daughter-in-law Maria, the wife of Paul, started this official department dealing with education, because we were obviously very behind in education in Russia at that time. The first was a small convent school; the second one was on exactly the same lines, and that's why they called it the St Catherine Institute, in honour of Catherine II. It was, I suppose, started very much along the lines of the schools in France and of foreign schools in general. They brought in the central curriculum[12] for all the schools, including the military schools for the boys and the various boys' boarding schools that were in St Petersburg, so the Institute's programme was adjusted. They had a central curriculum, like the one that they're writing here, only in Russia it happened about 100 years ago or more. People who don't have any idea about Russia think that they were all illiterate, and in some ways of course it was very restricted. Only a very small percentage of people profited by it; it was very unfair. But at least a start was made, and we had some very very outstanding educationalists at that time.

My parents didn't have to pay for my education because I was a ward of the Emperor; it was awarded to my father for his services on the royal yacht and so on. It means that the Tsar paid for everything. Half of the children in the Institute were *na kazenny schet*, paid for by various organisations or by the government. And then some of them were attached to the court and so on, things like that. So, it didn't cost them anything at all; we were fed and dressed, and on the whole quite well educated.

The girls went on to higher education like the boys if they wanted to. They had to stay on a year and do their Latin. We had these Bestuzhevskiye Kursy,[13] where the girls attended their own lectures but they had to pass their exams with the boys. Most of the people you meet now of my generation, who had been to university in Russia, had to go to these Bestuzhevskiye Kursy and pass their exams with the others. Bestuzhev was obviously some academician who had started these courses for girls and they were run on the same lines as the boys who were at university. I think it was mainly keeping the girls away from politics, because as soon as you entered the university, you immediately became political; it was very dangerous at that time. But, as I say, they had to pass the same examination for their finals. In the Bestuzhev courses there were only girls; the idea was not to mix with all these young men who were so political – like my husband. Probably they must have had some of them the same lecturers.

I was a boarder at the Institute; we had dormitories, bleak, oh pretty bleak, but I don't know, somehow we enjoyed it. We had a long dormitory, especially the juniors like me. Later on as you got to the higher forms there you had better beds and they were separated a bit one from another. But we just had rows of beds in a room. We always had the class madam, the class mistresses who looked after each girl. And we had two for each form, one who had to be German and one had to be French. And then when the French one was on duty you had to speak French to her and German to the German one. It was wonderful, and some of the girls who perhaps hadn't had as many governesses as others when younger all learnt to speak both languages. Very rarely you'd have a Russian class mistress. One of ours was Petz, and Petz was an Estonian and came from the Baltics. The Baltics used to provide us with many teachers. Another one was a Russian; she was Kuzmina. She was rather a bad-tempered old thing, but we were always teasing her.

We were taught the general subjects at the Institute. I was only in the juniors; I never finished my education there because of the 1914 war. So we did Russian, French and German for which you had to do both literature and dictation. We did mathematics and we had already started physics I remember because were going to the laboratory when I was about 13 or 14. We did chemistry and of course history and geography. People came in to teach us and the class mistress sat in the corner at her little desk to see that we behaved ourselves. Of course we very often had male teachers who came. We had quite a lot of dancing and singing, and in my time they had already brought in physical culture, you know, like PT and gymnastics. And of course an awful lot of music; our main music teacher was called Bach, Konstantin Bach. One of the great-great-grandchildren of Johann Sebastian Bach, but Bach was supposed to have had about a dozen illegitimate children anyway. Probably this one was legitimate because he had the name. And under him were a number of women music teachers. Of course they're a type of their own. And there was always an awful lot of intrigue going on because some who liked him stood up for him, and others were against him and didn't really agree with him. He obviously taught in other schools, possibly even in the theatrical schools as well. He had sideboards; he was quite an elderly man. Very Germanic. I think he spoke Russian. But I know that we had another teacher, my sister and I, whom for some reason my mother liked and wanted her to go on giving us piano lessons and she was always quarrelling with old Bach. They built on a musical wing at the Institute, which I remember very well. It was a little like opening the door and coming into swimming baths. And there was a sort of a special resonance in it I remember. Going into this wing right and left were cubicles with a piano in each where we had to practise, and some of them where lessons were going on. And as you came in there you heard scales going one side and something else being played somewhere else you know.

The school itself is on the Fontanka. It's still there; somebody brought me a photograph of it three or four weeks ago. She said:

'Oh I've brought you your school.' It was on the Fontanka opposite to Shuvalov's house,[14] and the Shuvalovs' house is now the House of Friendship with foreign countries. It was a very disciplined atmosphere at school. It wasn't so much working hard, as following a very strict, definite timetable. You all had to get up at the same time; there was a bell ringing and by the sound of the second bell we had to be all ready, washed and dressed. We used to lace each other's pinafores up. There was tea in the mornings, never any coffee, with *bulochka*, a little roll. And then lunch was at twelve o'clock – meat and vegetables. There was a big refectory, each form had its own table, and then after lunch we all had to go for a walk in the garden. Pretty boring; we had to put on our long coats and little caps and off we went. It was a nice garden, the back of it actually led on to the Liteiny Prospekt. And we just walked round, talked to each other I think. We had a small skating rink there for the winter, and a few things like the *pas de géants*. They had these in all the Russian parks. There's a big post in the middle that turns and loops are attached to it by heavy ropes. It goes round and you go round as it goes faster. It's like a roundabout, but as you go round the ropes get tighter and tighter and you fly up in the air. A sort of a whirligig. Some were little ones, with just three or four places for small children, and some were quite big. Of course there were various things that you weren't allowed to do because if you tried to pass somebody else and catch on to another rope when it went very fast it upset the balance.

After the park we came back for afternoon lessons and then we had supper at six o'clock, very early. After supper we were allowed to eat sweets, but until then it was forbidden. When supper was over, whoever the girl was on duty would go out and bring in a big basket where we had to deposit our sweets. There were an awful lot of sweets because it was a sort of tradition for anybody who went to the Institute to visit these 'poor girls' to bring some. We were terribly spoiled about them and so fussy, and knew all the newest makes of sweets in Petersburg. And there were quite a few very lovely boxes and so on, with chocolates. All were marked with our names and the basket was brought to each table. We could offer sweets to our friends but we didn't have to share. Then the basket was taken away and after that we had an hour or more in the big hall, and we had a very large hall, you know with a very polished floor, and we used to walk about there, talk and play games. I've forgotten if there were eight or ten windows looking on to the Fontanka, and that's where we got behind the curtains so that they couldn't seen us from the inside, and watched people skating. There was a big rink there. The Fontanka was a tributary of the Neva. So there were men and girls and skating around like this, and we used to watch and envy them sometimes. There was music playing, of course they had an orchestra, and all sorts of lights, fairy lights. Sometimes one of our class mistresses would get it into her head to come and see if anybody was there behind the curtain and get us all out and chase us back into the room, but it was all very friendly. There was this general feeling of belonging I think. I must say each form kept to itself and different girls had their best friends, but on the whole there was very much a feeling of loyalty to one's form, and each stood up for it. We had various performances, and put on plays. What really broke our monotony was when we were visited by somebody from the royal family. Usually it was the Dowager Empress[15] who used to come and see us or sometimes the Tsar. But whenever anybody came there was a very special bell that was only rung when there was a royal visit, and it rang right through the whole building, so we knew somebody had come. When the Dowager Empress last came, I was in the sanatorium with measles and could only hear the bell in the distance. But I never saw the Tsar. I saw him when we were in Peterhof at the parades.

Of course the great event of our school was our annual ball which everybody knew about in Petersburg, and that was at the end of November on St Catherine's day. The boys from the military academy came and that was all so exciting as you can imagine. I was there but I wasn't allowed to dance. I was in the junior form you see. Our forms started with numbers seven and six, five, four, three, two, one. And I was at the school only up to form four. I think it was the seniors, from classes three up to one, who were allowed to dance. We just had to sit round. We went in our uniform but our uniform was different; we didn't wear capes and I think the dresses were cut lower. They had something around the *décolletage* but otherwise it was the same. Then the different men's colleges arrived; sometimes some of the girls had brothers or something like that. Otherwise it was the military schools, the naval schools, and of course the *Corps des Pages*[16] who were the most brilliant of the lot. They came in their parade uniforms, a lot of white and red and gold, terribly glamorous.

Funnily enough, many years later I met somebody who said 'Oh I remember in November when they picked out the boys who were going to the Institute ball.' So they remembered, some had been allowed and some not. They were picked out to come and dance, but the young boys weren't allowed to come either, so they were always the senior forms of these schools, and we just sat and watched. I thought, 'Oh well, next year I shall be able to dance.' Well, next year never happened. The dances were all the ballroom dances of that period, and of course we loved waltzing and mazurkas, terribly exciting watching who's going to start the mazurka, who's going to do this or that, you know. And we all had our favourites among the senior girls in the top forms and so on, and we all argued about who were the pretty ones. Can you imagine? But then we did have a very good supper afterwards; we were always given *mors* to drink – it's a drink made from cranberries – and we had sandwiches and also *pirozhki*[17] of course. So we were given the sort of supper the others would be given, but we weren't allowed to dance. Sometimes there were a few young officers as well and that was always noted and watched. Usually they were either somebody special, or somebody's brother who had already graduated. So that was the great game, at the end of November. It was very nice because you know at the darkest, dullest time, we had orchestras.

I was also too young for the other entertainment at school, which was the Mariinsky ballet, and which the older forms went to. They went to the opera and ballet and they had a box next to the royal box you see. The royal box was in the middle and then the Smolnyi[18] girls sat on the right and we were on the left. The little ones didn't go, but we did go in the holidays. For our Christmas and Easter holidays we didn't come back to England because we only had a fortnight and so my parents didn't think it was worthwhile. We stayed in St Petersburg with friends, who of course spoiled us terribly and took us out all the time. It was actually my sister's best friend's family, the Filippovs, and they were always thinking up entertainments for us during that fortnight, having these two wretched girls staying. I remember going to the Kirov theatre and ballet very well; at the opera there were always two young guardsmen standing on duty outside the royal box at the back, and the idea was to pass him and either to make him smile, or to say something stupid.

When war broke out in 1914 we were here, in England. We

came back in May, our term ended and my sister had finished. They didn't want to send me back alone when the war broke out, because the only way to get back to Russia was through Scandinavia; the whole of the Continent was cut off. And that is when they sent me to the French lycée in London.

After I left school, well that was the Revolution. Everything collapsed, everything changed, everything became very different. I think at the time, in 1917, I was still at the lycée. I must have been 16 then and still at school doing my exams, but I went to teach French in an English school. For about a year and a half my father was still paid from Russia; there were funds. Whatever government money was here was put into a fund and people were paid so much a month while it lasted. The house we occupied belonged to the embassy, and had to be given up, the staff were dismissed and most of the furniture went to auction.

I met my husband when I was 19 and we were married a year later, in 1921. Oh he was a revolutionary of course and terribly romantic. Actually my father met him somewhere, he was a mining engineer by profession, and he had been in Siberia for a number of years. He really only came out with the Revolution. He was also mixed up with the SRs you know, Social Revolutionaries,[19] and so he left the country by travelling through Siberia and lived some time in Japan and in a sort of roundabout way came to England. But his main reason for leaving was to take out this old revolutionary, Ekaterina Breshko-Breshkovskaya. She was a very well-known person, actually quite famous and an extraordinary woman. She was known at that time as the *Babushka Russkoi Revolutsii*, the grandmother of the Russian Revolution. She had spent about fifty years in prisons in exile, and she only came out after the Revolution. As a matter of fact Solzhenitsyn writes about her in his book *1917*, how they're all expecting her back from Siberia, in great excitement. Some of these people there you see my husband knew, and so anyway she came back, and she was welcomed as a great heroine. But of course like all these old revolutionaries at the time, they were all welcomed and then they were all got rid of. And therefore she had to leave the country and my husband literally smuggled her out.

They travelled through Siberia when there was still the civil war on,[20] so they had to pass several fronts with a number of little primitive maps. From there she went on to the United States and she was very friendly with Herbert Hoover. She lived with the

Masaryk family in the United States until Tomas Masaryk[21] became the first President of the Czechoslovak Republic and brought her back with him. My husband couldn't go to the USA because they wouldn't give him a visa or something; I've forgotten why, but anyway, I might not have met him if he had.

When I look back on my life, I really missed the drama of the Revolution because I was here all the time. I remember I was very excited when my eldest brother came back because he was in the White army and we practically had no news of him for about five years after the Revolution. But then when he came back, although I was very excited and pleased to see him, I was already married, so you see I had other interests. Moreover he was very much the White army and I had a revolutionary husband and I was going off to Prague to consort with all those revolutionaries.

PRINCESS SOPHIA WACZNADZE

Princess Sophia Wacznadze was born Sophia Pestereff on 6 May 1908. Her father was a coal mining engineer in the Donetsk region of southern Russia. The family – of four girls and one boy – spent three years travelling to different White-held regions of Russia after the Revolution. In 1921, their British governess Helen Clarke secured them a passage to England. In 1944 Sophia married a Georgian, Prince David Wacznadze – a cartographer. Widowed for 15 years, with one son, Sophia Wacznadze now lives in Ealing with a friend.

My grandfather found coal. It's the Don basin; the agricultural workers on his estate were digging a well, just plain digging a well, and one fine morning they came up to his house, on to the porch, and emptied a bucket of coal in front of my grandfather. In those days it of course was something; it meant very hard work. My family lived there, and established the mines, which are there to this time, very close to Donetsk.[1] Those lands were Crown lands, because they were taken over during Catherine the Great's time. We were four girls and one boy, but in our family very strangely, only the girls are inheritors, and the boys have to be given their portions separately. That happened long ago, through a great-grandmother, who tied the wealth to girls only.

The first thing that I can clearly remember is the beginning of the First World War. The war started the Bolshevik Revolution in our part of the world. Of course, relatives took part in the war, everybody was working for the war, the mothers and fathers. That went for mother as well, working in a hospital. I didn't see any fighting, I only heard about it from uncles, aunts and cousins, who took part in it. In 1917 we heard that the Tsar had abdicated, and on the whole nobody was worried very much; there was the first Kerensky Provisional Government,[2] and the war went on and so the work for the war went on as well.

That summer they sent the Serbian regiment to our estate for rest and reorganisation. They had fought on the Eastern Front, and were badly mauled in the fighting. That was May 1917; the officers were quartered in our summer house, and so my French governess Mademoiselle and I were sent there to be hostesses. And I had a most lovely time; the house ran on as usual, but imagine me, a little girl sitting at the head of the table, and the table could seat forty people. Mademoiselle sat at the other end and there were thirty-eight Serbian officers in between; it was a glorious time, I tell you, so amusing. And to add to the fun of that May, I married off Mademoiselle to the Captain.

Mademoiselle took me for walks of course, and we were escorted by the gallant Captain. Well, I could easily play a little bit away with my ball to encourage them. At the end of the month, I returned back to Kharkov,[3] to the parents. Everybody was busy and it was a little bit harder. Yes, the estate was working, so the cows were fed, the horses were fed, the land was ploughed with oxen, lovely grey oxen with big horns.

When did your life change?

With the Bolshevik takeover,[4] when suddenly every bank closed, not a penny to be got. Now what happens is this: we own two large mines. I should say they're about 1,200 men together; some are miners, some are working on the machinery. The end of the week comes, there's no money, nothing at all, and here they are, families and families, with not a penny to spend or buy anything. Well, they borrow from their neighbours, who are not miners, who are farmers, and who have something to give them you see for the time being, but then what? And by that time we had already moved to our little district town; it was called Bachmut, but now it's called Artemovsk.[5] And then the miners' labour committee says that they wish to get hold of the owner, that is my mother, and they announce that they're going to hold her for ransom of a million roubles. It came out as a proclamation, and notices all over the place and of course everybody knew us by sight. So we couldn't stay in Bachmut, and especially our mother. She went off and disappeared in Kharkov; it's a big town you see, she had an old nurse living there and she went and lived there. My father decided that we had to be got out of Bachmut as fast as

27

possible. So father took us to a little station some way right out of the town, and put us on one of these trains for Kharkov.

The real Revolution began when the war front broke, and the remaining soldiers came home.[6] With rifles in their hands, they start walking to go home. And therefore they walk they walk they walk, and the first lot they arrive in the village. 'Oh', everybody said, 'Oh the poor young things, you know, so hungry, so cold and wet and miserable.' Every person makes the biggest cauldron of borshch,[7] everybody brings whatever they've got, and on they go. Before they've turned round there's another lot coming. They still are sorry for the soldiers, they still do something and help them and on they go by the way, but after a bit everybody begins to hide everything they've got, because if the soldiers eat it all what are they going to do? It's the winter, you see, it was October/November the Revolution, when the front broke, so it is November beginning of December. And it isn't troops, it's just a horde of armed men. That is what nobody visualises. Now after walking along, some get to a station and of course they pile on any train that's passing, right? And it's absolutely crammed in, and quite a lot of people are also riding on the roof. Well, quite often when they arrive into a village and there's nothing for them, of course then the looting begins. When father put us on a train to get away, it was just such a train full, absolutely full of soldiers, and of course it went along slowly and stopped at every station. The Bolshevik Red Guards used to come through the train, to see if there were any White officers or any other useless elements there. And you know they used to drag them out of the train and shoot them on the platform. There were my two sisters and I, in a third-class carriage with hard benches and a shelf above. Three little girls sitting on the bench up above, and my younger sister said, 'Now, I think we're coming to a station, now all you girls (that's my elder sister and myself), gather your saliva, as much as you possibly can, full mouth. And then, as the Red Guards pass us, see that you spit right in the middle of their gun, because that way we'll save lives. Because when the gun's all wet inside, it won't shoot properly.'

We did our best to save lives. Whether it managed to save them or not I can't say, but we did our best. That train continued slowly for many hours and we did the same at every station that we stopped, until we arrived at Kharkov. When the train came in to the station there was a crowd of other people on the platform who were desperate to get on to it. And so we couldn't get off because there was such a press of people who felt that their life depended on them getting on to that train. Finally our father, who had arrived before us, smashed a window of the train, and we were passed out through it. We went to a house of some friends that we knew slightly. They occupied a big corner drawing room and beside it there was a small room like a kitchenette, a pantry and another little sleeping alcove. And in this place we lived with Miss Clarke, our British governess, who went very quickly to see the English consul and he very kindly put a notice on our door: 'Under the protection of the British consul'. So Miss Clarke and the children were safe there; we didn't see my father and mother at all. Occasionally in the evening when it was perfectly dark, father would come to see that we were all right, and to bring us food. We stayed put there; where our mother was somewhere in the town we don't know, and where father stayed we also didn't know. We stayed with our English governess Miss Clarke, from December to March 1918.

During that time, Kharkov came under the supervision of a very cruel communist of Polish extraction, Dzerzhinski.[8] He's famous, the founder of the KGB, and he began to clear the town from all anti-communist elements. That meant people were shot and executed right, left and centre. It was winter remember, and in the morning you saw the blood on the snow. And then in March, the Germans came right across southern Russia as far as the Caucasus.[9] And I mean they deserve praise because that army was of course a civilised army; it wasn't a Hitler army at all, it was the Imperial German army, and they gave everybody a respite from the executions. Law and order reigned until September, and during that year the Germans bought the harvest and they paid for it. But of course the pressure on the Western Front was getting very heavy for the Germans by September, and so they couldn't leave their occupying forces in the East. They began to draw them away. Our parents realised directly the Germans went away, the Bolsheviks would again be on top of us. It was no good staying where we were, so we evacuated ourselves to the Crimea.

Well, we went to Simferopol, in the middle of the Crimea, and that is where we heard of the armistice and that the war was ended. Miss Clarke was contacted by the British consul, and told to get herself to Sevastopol, which she did, without us. She was put on a British man-of-war, and taken back to London.

When we arrived the Crimea was mostly a White zone. The main White group was in the north Caucasus and the Don, where the Reds hadn't advanced yet to occupy the parts that the Germans had just left. We had a second cousin older than ourselves who had been one of the cadets in St Petersburg. When the Revolution began, he was home on leave and therefore he was not involved in the massacre of the cadets,[10] and he also moved towards the Crimea and joined the White armies that were already formed under Kornilov.[11] One of the days when we were in Simferopol, it so happened that he was passing by and he came in. He stayed overnight with us, and I'll always remember how we tried our hardest to make him alive again. He was exhausted, he was wet through, and he hadn't eaten for three days. As a little girl I remember how we all fed him, let him sleep, found clothes for him, and after he'd rested two days with us, he went back. A little later we heard that he was killed at one of the crossings of the Dnieper river, in a battle between the Whites and the Reds, and that is the last we saw of him.

Meanwhile, the Reds were advancing towards the Crimea, and so our family considered it was no good sitting in a silly trap which is the Crimea, when there was an opportunity of going where there was a stronger defence. Our family arranged with difficulty for us to go on a ship which was going from Sevastopol to Novorossiysk,[12] and so the family – father, mother and the five children – went off to Novorossiysk. The elder ones were all studying whatever books they had, but on the whole it was very quiet, and rather dull there. Now, we'd already been travelling from here to there, in various houses not our own, and each little girl had her little pillow *dumka*. That is a little pillow with some kind of very pretty covering to it, for girls usually pink, that you can put under your cheek wherever you are, and you can then think and sleep well. But it's a tradition that you have this little pillow. Now, we had of course a brother who came next, 7½, and he hadn't got a *dumka* and he felt bereft. You know they were instead of teddy bears and cuddly toys that other children have. And my brother had nothing, so the girls set to and thought, specially the next sister who has an inventive mind, that's the one you know who organises everybody, 'Now girls, prepare a very nice cover, any bits that we can find, and any bits that we can embroider.' And then I asked, 'What shall we put inside it?' And the same Lisa said, 'The solution is very simple, we need feathers inside, right.' So, very quietly one fine day the three girls went and caught the ducks which were in the garden at Novorossiysk, and we held them well by the beaks, so that they shouldn't quack and make an uproar, and we pulled out a good lot of feathers. Two of the ducks, they were nice and fluffy, and we got you see a little bit excited over the matter, and perhaps we removed rather too many round the neck and breast, so two of them looked half naked. All these feathers, lovely lovely feathers inside the little cover, sown up and given to my brother. He now had a *dumka*, but the landlady came down as usual to feed the hens and the ducks, and what does she see? Naked ducks! The drama was fearful. The landlady roared. The parents you know were responsible for such cruel and nasty children, destructive vandals. The ducks had to be bought unfortunately, and in fact finally we had them to eat. But you know, as a few days passed the little pillow, the *dumka*, began to stink, my brother complained that it smells, but we said 'Shut up, don't dare breathe a word, see all the unpleasantness and drama that we've just passed through. And you've got your *dumka*, just put it to one side until it gets better.'

In Novorossyisk we passed our school exams as we should do, and then it was 1919, and we came to the end of the summer. We have a letter from an uncle who had gone back to our estate in the Crimea and in this letter he writes: 'I looked into the cellars and I found that they are untouched. I've taken out one barrel of wine and I've sold it very well, and therefore I've hired the dacha of the big hotel, in the middle of Yalta, so I don't see why you've got to stay in Novorossiysk, because all the Crimea and well away to the north is already in the hands of the Whites. You'd much better come back.' So at the beginning of September we came back to Yalta; we lived in a dacha, looking at the sea.

That autumn was particularly nice. I remember it as the very best part of my life; it was lovely. Well the Crimea is rather like the south of France in character, with its trees and things like that. Although there were difficulties for the grown ups, for us children it was an ideal time. Whatever the week, Friday evening, Saturday morning we used to go from our dacha, crossing certain of the Tsar's lands, to our estate where that year the grapes were not harvested. In the uproar, there was nobody to work the vines and just imagine, vineyards and vineyards of lovely grapes, white and dark and all colours, and there you could go, spend your time as much as you liked. And on that estate also lived our grandmother, my father's mother with her daughter, and our old coachman who'd come with grandmother. One day he comes to my parents and he said 'Now, give me a cart and two good horses, write me a letter and I will go right back to Kharkov and I will fetch some of your things that you obviously need here, because you haven't got anything much with you, neither have the children.' So my father wrote a letter, 'Allow Nikita to take whatever he thinks necessary from the house.' He had that letter with him, a cart and two horses, and off he went, and we said goodbye to him. We were very fond of old Nikita; he was a very nice man, and off he went, and we thought well, he'll go back, he'll have two good horses and a good cart, he'll settle down, and he'll be all right in the country, where his relatives, his friends all are, much the best place for him to be in. And five weeks after, because the distance is very great you know, I should say two or three thousand miles, he came back with five huge old-fashioned trunks. He brought the things as he thought best from the house, which stood perfectly still as it was untouched. There'd been no looting, nothing at all, and he selected what he thought was suitable. He brought my mother's wedding dress, because obviously it will be needed for the girls, right? And then the girls must have their dowries, that is absolutely essential, so piles of sheets, piles of pillowcases, piles of table linen, all properly embroidered as they should be with the initials. Well I should say he must have brought fifty of these, as well as two or three tablecloths for a table that could seat forty. And he also brought us our furs; they were first-class furs, beautiful sable, and of course in Russia you didn't wear a fur coat like you do in England, with the fur outside, you have the coat made in cloth or, if it is an evening fur, it is velvet, and it is on the inside that you have the fur. Anyway two whole big trunks were full of these lovely furs. Well, it was all very nice, and we continued over that winter in Yalta and then the White campaign began to totter; it was beginning to die, because this was already the end of 1919 and the beginning of 1920.

My father thought the situation is getting a little bit dodgy, and during that time, the British occupied the oil fields of Azerbaijan, right through to Georgia and Batum,[13] because that is the end of the pipeline. Georgia was under the occupation of the British by the beginning of 1920, so the parents thought we could go there. They sold some of the barrels of wine, and with it they bought wheat, because that is a commodity you can sell easily anywhere at all. Then they hired a trawler, that is a large motor boat which has two large holds usually for fish, but they are large holds. There's a tiny little deck-house where the captain sleeps, and a tiny little hold in the front of the boat; there is also a little place where the crew's hammocks are suspended. Our family joined up with another family of five who also who wanted to get away. They found fishermen who were very willing to work the trawler, four of them. Now, of course there's nowhere for anybody to live on the boat, and they were aiming across the Black Sea to Batum, and it usually took three days from Yalta. They thought and they thought, and then they bought an old railway truck, just a plain truck, you know one of these square things with nothing inside, that they move horses, cattle, goods or anything else inside them, and they put this thing on the deck. Now inside that they made a large shelf at one end, a large shelf at the other end, and on these shelves they put mattresses. So the other family went on the two shelves on one side, we went to the two shelves on the other side inside the truck. For our aunt, they made her a little bunk in between, away from the door. And on 25 March 1920 we set sail; of course our holds were filled with wheat. We got as far as the evening of that day, sailing quite nicely. The engine was of course a coal engine, and there was enough coal for three days, or a little more perhaps until we got to Batum, and there you could recoal, and then the four-man crew would take the boat back again, because it wasn't bought, it was just hired.

On the evening of that first day we got straight into a Black Sea fog. Now the Black Sea is famous for its fogs. They are absolutely dense; you can't see anything at all – obviously you can't see the sky and our crew had no idea how to navigate if they can't see the direction by the sky. And there we were, a day's journey out from the shore, in the midst of this fog. Now, it's no good going on; we were going south, and very soon in that fog you don't know where south is, no such things as compasses on the boat. Very difficult, one has to be very careful not to get close to any land, because if you got near to any land the ship would be grabbed. So the thing to do is to advance somewhere into the sea keeping a sharp lookout that you're not hearing anything like waves on a shore, and hope for the best. And for three days we went round and round in circles. That's what you do; you think you are going straight, but you're not, you're going round and round. Round and round for three days and three nights we went, of course

33

burning the coal that was supposed to take us to Batum. At the end of three days, the fog lifted and we were in the middle of the sea; you could see where east, west, south and north were. But practically all the coal was gone. Luckily my father is a mining engineer, so few things were hidden from him, and he said 'Well, there's very little coal left, what there is we'll use to go directly south and hit the Turkish coast somewhere. Meantime we'll use the wheat.' So, wheat was put in the furnace with the remains of the coal and off we went due south. Finally after days burning wheat, we arrived at a small fishing village of Sinop;[14] it's now quite a biggish town, but then it was a small place. There we downed anchor, and the men went off to see what kind of fuel they could get, and the most important thing, water. So the men arrived in Sinop and say 'Well, can you sell us some water first?' 'Sorry no, there's been a drought, we have no wells in Sinop, the only water that there is is in the cisterns and all our cisterns are practically dry; we can't let you have any of it.' Well, next thing 'Have you got any kind of fuel, kerosene and oil, perhaps you have charcoal?' 'No, no, no.' At last one person says 'Oil, oil, oil, the only thing we've got is some barrels of dolphin oil.' 'Dolphin oil . . . right, how many barrels have you got, we'll have them.' So dolphin oil was bought in barrels, wooden barrels, and then there was the big business of taking it on board. And when they were being winched aboard, one of these barrels slipped from its noose, and fell bang on the deck and split. And out came the oil, dolphin oil; it smells like horrible fish and rotten eggs, frightful.

The deck was cleansed as best it could be with sea water. But of course it stays smelly and slippery like nobody knows what. Never mind, our engineers improve the boiler again in some way, and by dipping sack in oil, it makes a kind of wick and you light it and it burns and the boiler goes, and the ship goes. And off we started burning this oil, but strangely enough when you burn it, it makes horrible large soots, like a candle, when it isn't burning very well and you see the black carbon. The smelly oil of course is ten times worse burning, and out of the funnel come huge soots – the size of an old half a crown. And of course they're heavy, they can't go far, they come floating down on the deck and sit on to this oily place. All children were confined to the inside truck; nobody was allowed to come out at all, but of course the thing to do is to dare somebody to step outside because it was like an ice rink. Directly you step outside you couldn't stand, your feet went both ways, and you went down flat on your hands like that. The children were doing their utmost to get victims out there and then haul them back. All these hands were absolutely black, oily black, and nothing to take it off with. All kinds of paper was used up, you know, doing the best one could. But we kept on chugging along, and finally arrived at Trabazon;[15] it's in Turkey.

Trabazon is quite a biggish town; it's a real port, and it has Roman baths, with natural warm springs, so directly we arrive there the whole lot of us went straight to these baths and spent the whole day getting ourselves purified, because we smelt to high heaven. Rotten eggs and fish, rotten fish, you can just imagine, but it was lovely. The water is so lovely and warm and finally you go into a warm swimming pool; it's gorgeous, and all inlaid with mosaic. So after we got out of there, we got proper fuel and went on to Batum. In Batum we disembarked and the wheat was sold, so money was available. In the country outside Batum, in a place called Chakva,[16] along the coast, there were experimental tea plantations. Now, they've become huge tea-growing places, but in those days it was only a small place, on the railway, and the tea plantation was in the hands of a Chinaman, who disappeared during the Revolution. He had a bungalow there which stood empty. And this bungalow was hired by our family, and the very smallest amount of furniture put in, chiefly bamboo, which grew locally.

So, to Chakva we went and started living there. And there our old governess, Miss Clarke, found us. One fine day, we have a letter, a piece of paper under the door, on which is written in English, 'Miss Helen Clarke would like to know how you all are?' Just like that. 'If you'd like to answer her, would you please put your letter under a stone by the milepost on the main road.' So my mother writes in English, 'We are very happy to hear that you, Miss Clarke, are all right; we are all all right, the whole family is here, and so nice to hear something from you.' And then that letter is put under the stone by the milepost that's down our hill, and there the main road passes. Well, about a fortnight later we had another little letter underneath the door, and this time 'Miss Helen Clarke would like to know if you would like to come to England.' So another long letter is written; yes how much we'd like to come to England, how good it will be for the education of the children, this that and the other, and it is put under the stone by the post. And then nothing again, and then after some time, a knock on the door, late in the evening when it was already dark, and then a voice says, in English, 'I come from Miss Helen Clarke, may I come in?' We opened the door, and there stands a Kurd. And he said 'I understand that you'd like to go to England; I'd like to know the full particulars of all your family, names, ages and everything like that, and you see arrangements will be made.' So a whole list of who we were, father, mother and all the children. And our aunt was also with us, my mother's sister; all were put down, and he said, 'Presently I will be in contact with you again, but you must be ready to go within an hour when we come for you.'

So there we sit for a little longer and then one evening, it was already December 1920, again they arrive in the middle of the night, two o'clock and a knock at the door and again, 'I come from Miss Helen Clarke; in an hour we will come and fetch you – get ready.' Up everybody in the middle of the night, all get dressed, everything folded up and packed away, no mattresses, no beds, no nothing like that. But of course we had our pillows which were brought by the coachman, and then we sit and wait until exactly one hour, three o'clock in the morning, knock knock at the door, door's opened wide and in come a horde of Kurds, pick up everything that there is there, including the younger children, and we go, down our little hill, across the main road, and then across the railway line, on to the beach. Straight on to the beach, and there was a motor boat in which the whole lot were piled in and taken out to sea. And a suitable distance apart was a cargo ship that usually goes from Istanbul to Trabazon and back again, carrying passengers and goods. But then it stood empty for us, and we were put aboard along a rope, very handy sailors I must say, one behind each person to push them up from behind while they're climbing, and then you feel quite safe. And there we were with all our goods on board this ship that went straight to Trabazon to collect its usual passengers and goods. And the goods that time were chiefly sheep, the whole of one deck was full of sheep, and figs. Bags of figs, and certain of the bags had little holes in them, so it was very entertaining whilst we were on deck – to while away the time you could pinch a dried fig out of the little holes. You know mice could do it quite easily. We arrived at Istanbul, and directly we came inside the Bosphorus, the British admiral's yacht with Miss Clarke on board came to meet the ship. Were we pleased to see her? Oh dear me, we were so delighted.

And without any customs, without anything, with many apologies from certain people: 'We're very very sorry. Because the evacuation of the Crimea has just been completed, and Istanbul is chock a block with refugees, we've had to put you in two hotels. Please forgive us!'

We were in one hotel, and father and mother and the younger boy and girl were in another hotel. And then more apologies and excuses because of the situation: 'There's very little shipping at the moment; we're very sorry, but you'll have to stay here for a week or two.' So we were in Istanbul for about a fortnight. And then a P&O boat that was under government orders to go to Alexandria in Egypt to evacuate British in hospitals, called at Istanbul and picked us up. So we got the P&O boat, and went to Alexandria, where we got hold of all the goods and of a field hospital, a military hospital; I think there were about twenty nurses, and six or seven doctors, and all their goods that were packed. In fact, in Alexandria we stayed three days so we could have a little look at the town meantime.

From there straightaway we went to Malta, where this hospital and these personnel were taken off and remained in Malta, and again we stayed there about three days, and on we went next to Gibraltar where the same thing happened. And then we started round by the Bay of Biscay and arrived in Britain on 4 January 1921, Tilbury Docks, where we were all piled into taxis and we went under Big Ben. We stayed with Miss Clarke's parents in Hunstanton. Now, all kinds of things that could possibly be sold were sold, including the furs, which filled some of those big trunks. And Miss Clarke's brother had a large farm near Wisbech, in the fruit-growing district. With the help of Miss Clarke's brother, and the money that we finally gathered together, we bought a five-acre orchard that was already planted with apples, plums and strawberries. It was decided that my father would build a house there, because being an engineer he had the know-how; he had one labourer to help him and he built our house in Wisbech-St-Mary. With, mind you, a loo and running water; nobody in the whole village, including the biggest landowner or the vicarage, had such a thing. And so in the summer of 1922 the family moved into residence there. And some of us remained in the house until just the first year of the Second World War.

We all went to school, of course; the advantage we all had was that we could all speak English, so it was no great difficulty. My

37

youngest sister was 5 and started school in the infants. She had the greatest advantage in her scholastic career because in the middle of the day, her best friends, those who brought her apples or something sweeter to eat, were allowed to walk home with her and pull the loo chain! – such a waterfall had never been seen.

DOROTHY RUSSELL

Dorothy Russell was born on 20 March 1905. Her father, Frank Cooke, had been tutor to the Grand Duke Dmitri,[1] and Prince Felix Yusupov. He was later imprisoned, and the rest of the family were forced to work in Moscow to survive during the Revolution. She married William Russell in 1931; they had one son and one daughter. Widowed six years ago, she now works as a sculptor in Essex.

My sister and I were born in St Petersburg, and then we moved to Moscow when I was two. Finally we moved to a lovely big house in a village about fifty miles away from Moscow. We had a manservant there, and two other servants and a huge garden, and instead of a refrigerator they built a hut under some trees and dug a deep hole, and then put a ladder in this hole and filled it with snow, and that lasted the whole summer. It's very hot in Russia in the summer, but you put all the things on to the snow. We used to hire a horse and a sledge, and then we children would drive, and we'd turn a sharp corner, so that the sledge would turn over and everybody would be in the snow, and we thought that was great fun. And my uncle lived not very far away. He had two pure arab horses; they were like a troika,[2] the centre one looks forward and the other to the side – one of them looked to the right. I used to ride on them bareback; it was a bit scary, because sometimes the horse wouldn't want to go out. And once it came back it started galloping, and when you've only got the reins and no saddle it's difficult for a child.

At the age of 7 we moved back to Moscow, and we went to a German school; at our house we used to have a German governess and we spoke German to her, English to my parents and Russian to everybody else. Then later on I went to France for twelve years. And it's funny because when I'm speaking English, when I meet strangers, they always ask me 'Now, what nationality are you?' And I'm English. Both my parents were English – although I was born in Russia, I'm of English stock. But I roll my 'r's and that gives me away.

In this German school, everything was very, very hard discipline – just not allowed. They had a big hall for each four classes, and you weren't allowed to run in that hall at all, or speak. And then in 1914 when the First World War broke out, we left that school because German was a dangerous language to speak in the street; we weren't very welcome. And so we went to a Russian school, and there we had to curtsey every time we met the headmistress in the corridor. When the Revolution came this school was joined on to a boys' school, the classes were divided into very big classes, fifty in each class, and my sister was the president of her class and I was the president of my class.

One day it was Christmas time and there were two geese in the school. By this time food was extremely short, and we had 2 ounces of bread a day, for which we had to queue. It was 1917, and my mother used to teach English at my school, and so my mother, my sister and I, and another girl, were all in the larder together where there were two geese – two geese for 176 pupils. Imagine how much we got. But anyway we never got any because those geese were stolen. And my mother and sister and I, because we had been in the larder, were accused of stealing the geese. Well, my sister is very self-contained, and she could control herself, and she had to sit in the room, and she was just very pale and sat perfectly still without saying anything. Well you see I am different; I was so furious I just couldn't contain myself. I was aged 13, and I got up and I just burst out, said 'You have no right to accuse us of stealing those geese just because the three of us were there; you have no proof at all.' And I really just let go. I can't remember what else I said but I know that I was absolutely furious and I stayed at that school for another fortnight or so, but it really was a terrific strain on me because teachers always used to say 'Well, it does look likely that you've taken them, there are three of you,' and it got too much for me; anyway, to cut this story short, many months later the other girl who was with us confessed to having stolen them. But I left the school and I went to a little factory, to knit stockings, blue and red stockings, and there were about a dozen girls working there. I had to get some food someway; I was earning nothing but a plate of soup – from eight to twelve I worked, and for that I got a plate of soup, and that's all. My sister was doing something else; she was putting powders into papers in a medical place.

We couldn't get out of Russia. We had to go to a certain place to check up when we were going; it was all done through the Red Cross. When finally we went, we got three days' notice. When we had been in our first house, in the big one, we had a servant, and she was called Pasha and she was particularly fond of me, and she was such a nice woman, and when we went finally I gave Pasha two lovely dolls, and I always remember the words I said to her, 'Pasha, keep these for me and one day I'll come back.' And of course that was impossible; I don't even know her surname or anything so there was no way of ever coming to find her, and I don't know what she did with those dolls. I had a great affection for her, but there was another nurse that we had long before, when we were still in Moscow, when I was only 3 and she was our first nursemaid and her name was Dulichka. She came straight from an orphanage to us, and she was an awfully nice person; we loved her. Then, when I left Russia and I was living in Paris, my sister-in-law was living in a big block of flats, and she heard of a Russian woman there, and she found out, and it was Dulichka. And the first thing she asked me was 'How old are you?, because I only know my age by your age.'

What do you remember of the Revolution?

I can't really say that I remember a great deal, but it was dangerous to go out into the street. We lived very near to the barracks, and one day when the Revolution was in full swing, at one o'clock in the morning we heard terrible bangings on the front door. We never used the front door, because it let too much cold air into the flat, and it was so cold in the flat that if you poured out a hot cup of coffee, in five minutes there would be ice on it. That's what we had to live with; quite often we had to sleep in our coats, you know, and have a hat on our heads to keep warm. But this time there was this terrific banging on the door and we knew it was soldiers, and they came to fetch my father, because he was English. They searched the whole flat, and father was put into the Butyrki,[3] that's the central prison, and there were a whole lot of murderers and thieves there. And when they called out a name, a man would take his belongings, and as he was going out they'd shoot him. My father had two nasty gashes on his leg, very bad, and he had to have them treated by a doctor and the doctor shouted at him like anything, calling him every name conceivable, and then when the guards were a short distance away from him, the doctor then said 'Mr Cooke, I'll do everything I can for you; I was one of your pupils, but I don't want the guard to know.' But he couldn't do anything much unfortunately because father was transferred. He was transferred to a monastery because it had higher walls and he couldn't escape. And you see we didn't know where he was, we just knew he'd been transferred, and he had to walk from the Butyrki to this monastery, three miles in the middle of winter, with just bandages on his feet. And when he collapsed in the road, absolutely exhausted, a soldier stuck a bayonet in his ribs and said 'Get up you dog or I'll shoot you,' and so he had to struggle and go on; how he did it he didn't know. And there he was put in this monastery, in a cell, and they got in as many beds as they could into this cell, and they had a terrible time, and the food was absolutely appalling, it really was. They were covered with bugs and lice, and they used to catch the bugs and put them over a candle to hear them go pop, just for something to do.

We started looking for him. We went to several monasteries, and we came to this one at last, and it had a huge wrought iron gate, and then a short distance beyond a small doorway, and you could see a whole lot of men straining to see who it was who had come. And I said to my sister, 'I'm sure I saw Daddy!' And we waited outside for two and half hours in the bitterest of bitter cold weathers, and I remember the date – 21 December 1919, it was my father's birthday. And after waiting there for two and a half hours, we ran to the door, and it was my father. And he cried, and we cried, and even now, all these years later, it's all I can do to fight my tears back, because I can relive it; it really was absolutely unforgettable. And after that we used to go and see him every Sunday, and he would be given a tin of condensed milk by the Red Cross, and he'd give us a piece of black bread about an inch square with a few drops of condensed milk, and that was our treat for the week. And my sister always said that when she got free she would have quite a lot of condensed milk. She did, and she was sick, and she never had any afterwards.

While father was in prison, our days were really spent in queuing up for various things. And you know 2 ounces of bread isn't very much. Sometimes we bought bread on the black market; mother got some once and it was so awful that she gave a piece of it to a friend of the family, a doctor, and he discovered that it was 95 per cent other matter, including old soldiers' coats and dust from the road, and only 5 per cent flour. That's what we had to eat. We bought one loaf, and paid quite a lot of money, but we couldn't even cut it with a chopper.

Apart from bread, we had things fried in cod-liver oil and castor oil. Mother once bought twelve dozen eggs from a salesman, and she picked out five that were good; the rest were rotten, really rotten – they stank to high heaven. And we went on and on breaking them, hoping to get one. Frying things in castor oil isn't very tasty, and we used to have to fry the potatoes, frozen potato ends, and they're slimy and horrible. There was so little to eat that we were really very, very hungry. When I was working in this place with the girls, knitting stockings, I suddenly felt terribly ill, and I fell on to my machine, and I was taken out. They had to get a stretcher, and people seeing me carried out like that on the stretcher thought it was a corpse but I'm still here. Then another time in Moscow, in the same place, I was standing holding two pieces of bread in my hands, one for my sister and one for myself, and a boy came and snatched them away from me. Quick as lightning I caught hold of the boy by the scruff of his neck, and I started shouting for all I was worth for help. The officials came and started searching the boy, and found he'd got seventeen bread loaves, so they took the whole lot away. And a little girl came up to me and said 'That boy belongs to a gang, and they're conspiring to beat you.' So I thought discretion was the better part of valour, and I made myself scarce. The next day, I went and claimed that bread and I got the two pieces back. But for that, every time I came into the canteen, I'd look round the room first, to see that there wasn't a gang waiting, because I don't know what they would have done to me if they'd caught me. The canteens were run by the government. They were set up for children; you had to have ration books, and you were given a plate of soup and a piece of bread.

Mother worked from eight in the morning till eight o'clock at night; she had to walk everywhere, and her classes were quite a distance. She had to work, and she was very, very tired at the end of the day. She taught Russian soldiers; some of them were just raw peasants and they had no education at all, and to go into a class with fifty of these men was quite hard. She was very small, but she had a wonderful character, and the soldiers really loved her.

In Moscow we had a flat with five rooms, and there were just three children and mother, so they said that we had to give two rooms to others. We had a woman from the Baltics, and her three sons, teenagers, and they were all thieves. They just got into our part of the flat, got the key, and they stole things, and we had a big volume of Pushkin, the poet, and we missed it, and we asked them if they had it and they said no they hadn't. Well, a bed divided the room between us and the family, and I dropped something under the bed once, and I climbed under the bed, and under I could see the Pushkin volume in that part of the flat. This woman would sell things for my mother on the black market, and I would go too. It was a huge market; it was about a mile or two long, and you could get absolutely everything there. She would always tell me to go away from her and sell our goods in another place, and then she would tell mother a different price to what she really got for it. And here I did a thing that I was always terribly ashamed of, and it was years before I confessed it to my mother. One day I saw some very nice hot food there, and I bought it, and I told mother that I'd got less for the thing that I'd sold than I really had, and I have this terrible guilt. One day when we got back to England I told her the truth, and she said 'For heaven's sake why didn't you tell me just the price and then I wouldn't have said anything.' The Bolsheviks didn't want this market to take place, so they used to raid it, and the soldiers with red caps would catch everybody that they could and then send them to prison. Well when I was there they had a raid. There were a whole lot of men with red caps on, and I remember hesitating because there was a great big puddle in front of me, and I didn't want to go into it, and then a hand in the back picked me up and pushed me. It was just a peasant boy who saw me hesitating.

Finally though our life in Moscow ended because the Red Cross arranged for us to get out of Russia, and my father was let out of prison the day before we left for England.[4] We left by train from Moscow, and went to the Russian/Finnish border; there was a board laid across a small ravine, and on the other side was Finland. And the Commissar stood in the middle of this board and shook hands with every person and I remember standing on the Russian side, and being so afraid that the board would break before it was my turn. When the soldiers crossed over, the British Red Cross was there to meet them and take them off; they had Union Jacks and we were all waving frantically. And we were all given Ovaltine and things like that, as much as you liked. I just had one cup; my father had eight. It was lovely. And then we were given peas to eat; that's a funny thing to give somebody who's not had much food, peas in a vegetable dish, and you could have another one if you wanted. I went to ask for a second one, but I didn't really want it; it was simply the liberty involved in having another one. And then, when we were going past a shop in Finland, where you could buy things, and there were no queues, you know everybody went 'ooooooooh', like packs of wolves, and it sounded like we were starving.

We arrived on a Finnish bank holiday, and there were crowds and crowds of people in the street, because we were the first prisoners of war to come out of Russia. We met the British consul there, because mother knew him, and he treated us very well. All the soldiers and everybody went to a hotel and there was an orchestra and a balcony, and all the soldiers had been told to behave well. And they did, and when they started playing *Tipperary* the soldiers wanted to sing it, and so the band leader stopped the orchestra, and then he leant over the balcony, and he invited them to sing, and I've never heard *Tipperary* sung with so much feeling. You know the crowds outside heard it, and they cheered, and then when we finished, had a lovely meal, we went back to the train, and the Finnish government had provided a parcel for every passenger and it was wonderful.

When we arrived in England, I had two impressions, one was good, one was bad: how green the grass was, that struck me so much; it was marvellous, and the grass was lovely and green, and you see we'd come from snow, but I didn't like the terraced houses. When we came into the Channel and saw the first cars and the cliffs of Dover, that was really thrilling, to know that you were in England. And then we went to stay in a hotel with my aunt, and she was French, and she was very popular in that hotel, and she told everybody about us coming, so when we came into the dining room, every head turned to look at us and very self-consciously we sat down, and my sister picked up the menu, and she said 'I can't read it; I don't know what it is.' So she said 'Well, we'll have some kippers.' Well, I had no idea what kippers were, and certainly had never had any kippers before, so when they came I went 'Ah', and the whole place laughed.

I've had some very exciting times, but I haven't mentioned my aunt, and I think I should, because this is a wonderful story. My aunt was a portrait artist, very clever, and she came to us when I was 7, to the big house and to the flat in Moscow too. She was very beautiful, and she had lovely rosy cheeks, and we always called her Aunt Rosy-cheeks. And she had lovely long hair, and she was very small and very jolly. She married a Russian, and she was accused of being a spy during the Revolution. She was taken to trial, and they said she must either become a spy for them or be shot on the spot. So with her head held high she walked out of that place. She said 'I will not be a spy,' so they commuted her death sentence to life imprisonment. First of all she spent three years in prison, and then she was taken in a cattle truck to Siberia. And in the cattle truck, some sat on the floor, some on the board half-way between the ceiling and the floor, for three weeks in the middle of winter. They were given very little food and no toilets or anything of that sort. And she arrived in Siberia and she spent twenty-three years there. And as she was a good artist, they made her paint portraits of Stalin, to put in the various offices and hotels and things like that. They had one master painting, and she had to copy that over and over again, so she got slightly better treatment than some of the other prisoners. In 1955 she was pardoned, and told that she was innocent. They couldn't give her back the twenty-three years of imprisonment. When I heard that she was pardoned and that she came to stay with her daughter in south Poland, I wanted to hear her story, and I didn't want to hear it in writing because it might be censored. I was 60 then and I'd never driven a car, so I bought a car and eighteen months after passing my test, I went to Poland. Drove to Poland by myself, and it was really exciting.

I got to the village, and saw my aunt. You know there are sixteen years difference between my aunt and my mother, and they weren't in the least bit alike when they were younger, but there was mother standing just as though she was there herself. They were so alike. Even her crooked little fingers. And I was completely at a loss for words.

IRINA SERGEVNA
TIDMARSH

Irina Sergevna Tidmarsh, the daughter of a social democrat and a lawyer, was brought up as a member of the intelligentsia in Moscow. Her brother fought for the White army and her father was imprisoned due to this and other anti-Bolshevik connections. In 1920 the family was smuggled out of Russia through the Polish frontier and Irina arrived in London aged 17.

I was born in Moscow in 1903. My mother at the time had a little flat in one of the old streets of Moscow, branching off the Arbat.[1] It was called Molchanovka. When I was born, my mother was living alone because she had separated from her first husband and wasn't yet married to my father. So I was really born out of wedlock, when my mother was 28. When things like that happen, according to the old Russian law, you had to be adopted by your father later on, which I was. My mother specialised in mathematics. She was a very good mathematician with a degree. She also had a child by her first marriage, Rafa, who lived with her, and she had to look after him. He went to school, and in Russia there were very few boarding schools, so he lived at home with her. She had quite a lot of people to look after him, because there was her old nanny, who had been nanny in their family for years, and also my aunt, who was known as Tetya Masha, and in the winter she always lived with us. She married quite late in life, and had no children. She was twenty years older than my mother and treated her like a daughter. When my mother was born, her mother died in childbirth. There was a great gap between the birth of her first children and the birth of my mother, and so the two elder daughters brought my mother up.

My mother's family was from the old Russian nobility. The Russian nobility was a bit different from the nobility in England because it was very widespread. The very old nobility mostly didn't even have titles. But there was a lot of created nobility during Catherine the Great's reign and most of them had some kind of title. They were either counts or princes and so on. As you know it was an agrarian country, so most of them had some kind of property in the country, not just around Moscow, but around the big towns as well. It was a country gentry. You had three classes in Russia; you either belonged to the nobility, or to the merchant class, or to the peasants and artisans. There were three different categories which were written down in your passport. But the intelligentsia consisted of educated people, who could belong to any class. It started in the 1860s, when people began to be educated, and lots of them came from the professional classes.

Before the Revolution we spent winters in Moscow and summers at an estate outside Moscow, called Belokolodez, which means white well. It wasn't really our family estate; it belonged to my aunt Masha. We spent six months there every summer, my mother and myself and numerous cousins. Belokolodez was surrounded by three large orchards, so there were always a great deal of apples of all kinds. There were a lot of soft fruit like currants, redcurrants, raspberries, strawberries and a large kitchen garden with all kinds of vegetables. There was a big poultry yard, and meat, pork and lamb. Only things like rice, porridge and semolina were bought outside the estate. It was bought in one of the two towns that were in the vicinity. One place, called Rouwhye, where there was a railway, was twenty-five versts from our estate; that's about twenty-seven miles. On the other side there was another railway station called Vino, at more or less the same distance. We were right in the middle there. Once every three months there was a large expedition to the town, to buy cereals and things that we didn't have, household foods that we were in need of. Otherwise it was all produced on the estate.

We had a coachman who was a drunkard, but he looked after all the horses. We had several horses; there was a troika, and there were at least four riding horses. I had my own pony called Zvezdochka, meaning little star, which I loved of course and rode every day. Then there was my brother's riding horse, and my mother's and my aunt's. There were also all kinds of horses that were used for labour; one old mare used to drag a big tub of water every evening so that the flowers could be watered in the garden.

As for domestics in the house, we had an old nanny who lived there. She didn't do any work; she was already very old indeed, and when I was still quite young she died. We always had a very good cook and a man who used to wash up. There was a big sandpit outside the kitchen window, and that's where he cleaned all the saucepans. Most of the saucepans were made out of brass and they had to be cleaned to look shiny. And then there were always two, sometimes even three maids; they always came from our village and were young girls. The older ones, who had been in service before, used to train the younger ones. They had a lovely room at one end of the house, looking out on to the garden. Then there was Doylia, the German governess, who really was like a housekeeper and looked after all the maids and all the provisions. She had lived in our house since mother was a child, and had helped to bring her up. She had the keys of the larder where all the food was kept. It had a lot of jams and marmalades, and Doylia used to love making them. In the garden she had a brick stove and she stood there for ages over a very large brass saucepan with a long wooden handle, and cooked all that fruit. It was a continuous occupation for her, and she always used to wear a little bun on top of her head.

The house was white with the family crest painted on the front. It was one storey but it was very long and there were eight bedrooms and two drawing rooms, a very large dining room and two studies. All this was on the first floor, and at the end there was a big door which led to the kitchen. There was a laundry room and quarters for the cook. Outside for the servants there was a very large nice wooden table with wooden benches, surrounded by acacia trees. The servants always used to have their meals out of doors, so they really didn't have a very bad life. Of course they had to work hard, and especially the maids because we always used to have all our meals out of doors as well. Only when it was raining did we have them in the dining room or in the covered terrace at the back of the house. There was an open terrace at the front of the house. I always remember how the maid used to come in the morning to my aunt and ask 'Where would you like your meals?' And according to the weather and Tetya Masha's will we had the meal wherever. We often had lunch under the oak tree or under the pine tree, or by the flower garden in front of the house. The poor maids had to carry enormous trays with all the crockery and all the silver and all the food outside. But it wasn't too bad; they didn't really mind.

Breakfast was generally served in the covered back terrace of the house. It was always lovely white homebaked bread, delicious, fresh out of the oven that same morning. And of course butter and a lot of different honeys. They came from our own apiary just outside the park, where an old man lived and looked after the bees. One kind of honey was very light and sweet-smelling; it was made from lime trees. Then there was another kind which was heavier and dark brown in colour, called *grechika*, which means buckwheat. Buckwheat is something that the Russian *kasha*[2] is also made out of.

About midday we had lunch. It always consisted of three dishes; first a light dish like rice made with herbs or else macaroni. Then there was either cold meat or fish which came from our pond, and was either boiled, roasted or fried. And then always a sweet dish which was usually *kisel*, which is a very runny, very liquid jelly. Then we used to have a light pastry filled with curd cheese which I loved, and with cream. And that was lunch. Everyone always used to have a rest after lunch, and we children went swimming. We were taken there in a little *tarantas* – a vehicle made out of plaited straw – and an old horse which took us to the river where we used to swim. The river was very narrow but quick-flowing; it was very deep and quite dangerous for children, so there were wooden structures by the water on the river bed which we held on to.

Coming home we were hungry and there was always something on the table for us – bread and butter, some cakes and milk. In the evening at seven o'clock there was a large meal which was the last meal of the day for the children. It was mostly served on the open terrace, and Tetya Masha used to sit at the head of the table with us all round, and numerous dogs that we had at the bottom of the terrace. The dogs all knew when the meal was on, and they lay there hoping for a titbit of some sort. None of the children ever dared throw anything to the dogs because there would be a fight. Once there was really an awful fight and my brother had to jump out from the table and managed to pour some water over the dogs to separate them.

Mr Silvester was my tutor at Belokolodez, and he used to be frightened by the dogs or any disturbance like that. He was very pernickety, moved slowly and hated any commotion. He was a very funny character. He had a bald head but he grew long tresses on either side and used to brush them up to cover the bald patch.

We children knew that he used to do this in his room in the morning, brushing the hair up to the right and to the left, and we used to love watching. There was a crack in the door so we used to sit there watching how Mr Silvester arranged his hair.

Anyway that was the end of the supper and after that we children always used to go riding. We'd go along the road to the edge of the river and I always remember the wonderful smell of mint there, and the peasants who used to have little straw huts on the edge of the river. Every evening they used to drag this mint out of the river banks, and the smell was absolutely wonderful. We rode in the fields and the woods and when we got home it was already bed-time. We had perhaps one biscuit but then most of us children were in bed by half-past nine. The grown ups sat on the terrace and they used to play an awful lot of Preference. Preference is a card game like bridge and my aunt was very fond of it. The priest of the local church on the estate used to come every evening to play this Preference.

The grown ups got to bed very late. The young people, my brother and a little German governess called Emma who was about 20, used to play the piano together, sing and go for walks. Well that went on till late at night and always at twelve o'clock they had supper. They mostly played bridge unless it was some kind of church holiday when you couldn't indulge in anything. They loved it.

We made ice-cream at the estate; we used to have a little hut built in the park and every winter they filled this hut with ice. There was no floor to the hut, it was just dug rather deeply so the ice went underground and was very thick. All round the hut were shelves, and on these shelves stood earthenware jars with all kinds of milks and creams and butter, and ice-cream made there by the cook who used to come and sit in the hut and turn around a machine to make it.

One summer at Belokolodez we were given a parrot. He arrived in a very tall cage standing on some kind of wooden platform and there was a little grey bird sitting inside called Popka. He called us all by our names very soon, and inside his cage there were grains he continually ate. He fluttered about the surrounds of his cage, but very soon we were disappointed in Popka because he wasn't a kind bird. He had a very large beak and black, piercing little eyes. Whenever we got near the cage, and somehow managed to put our fingers near the bars, he at once bit us and bit us very badly; it hurt. And he didn't have a very pleasant voice. Sometimes he screeched and screeched, a piercing awful sound that went through one's head. When we got fed up with him we used to cover his cage to keep him quiet. But on the whole he was very clever because whenever we had a new maid or a new cook, he learnt their name at once. Tetya Masha liked him and taught him to say 'Where are my spectacles? Where are my spectacles? Go and look for my spectacles.' She was always losing her spectacles and we children had to go and look for them, and Popka used to say 'Come on, come on, quickly, quickly! Look for the spectacles.'

Once a week Tetya Masha used to give Popka a bath. That was very interesting because she had a large spray affair she used to fill up with vodka, and then she used to spray him. Birds in little cages very often get insects in their feathers and so for hygienic reasons Tetya Masha sprayed him every week. Well, Popka didn't like it; he didn't like the vodka, but at the same time he also got quite drunk and he used to walk about his cage swaying from side to side. He would begin to swear at Tetya Masha with awful swear words that he learnt whilst he was on a naval boat. Tetya Masha was very prim and proper – she was the widow of a general – she didn't like that swearing and used to say 'Shut up Popka! Stop that swearing.' But that went on and on and she used to absolutely lose her temper. That was very interesting for us children, and we always used to watch the bathing.

When the weather was good, Popka was always put under a terrace that was at the back of the house. He used to sit there and of course he heard that there was a large poultry yard at the back of the house which was managed by a woman called Natasha. There were a lot of birds there and Natasha used to come out when it was feeding time and call 'tsyp-tsyp-tsyp' and all the birds would come. Popka started imitating her, and whenever he felt wicked he started to say 'tsyp-tsyp-tsyp'. His cage would be surrounded by squeaking chickens and geese and ducks and goodness knows what else, all the inhabitants of the poultry yard.

One day Popka managed somehow to escape from his cage. He flew right into the village, and at the outskirts there lived a little old woman in a little hut with a straw roof. Suddenly she heard a voice on the top of her roof. Through the chimney she heard a voice swearing like anything. She thought it was the devil so she ran out of the house shouting 'There's a devil on top of my roof.' All the peasants came running and they laughed; they knew that it was that little grey parrot that used to live in a cage in our house, so they managed to catch him and bring him back. And that was how Popka lived in our house for many years.

But then our lives were changed by the storm that was the Revolution. My father decided to emigrate and so a new home had to be found for Popka because we couldn't take him with us. We found a home for my little dog Flock, but we couldn't find anyone for Popka. Then some friends of ours told us about a man named Basov who worked in a circus. If Popka was intelligent enough he might join his circus team of animals. Basov duly arrived. He looked at Popka; he heard Popka say *'Popka durak, Popka durak'* (Popka is a fool). Then he took him away. A few weeks later before we left Russia, this Basov rang up my mother and said 'Will you come and visit Popka?' And he rang up my aunt as well; 'Will you come to see what I've managed to teach Popka?'

It really was a transformation when we got there. Popka was very fond of his new master, and when Basov whistled, Popka came out of his cage and flew to perch on his shoulder. Then Basov would say 'Now it's time for our singing lesson.' And what do you think? Popka would start singing all kinds of famous songs, for instance he sang *Gaida Troika*:[3] 'Hello horses, the snow is fluffy, the snow is white, let's go for a troika ride.' That's what happened to Popka. I think when we left Russia he was very old indeed; he must have been almost 90. But Basov made a famous bird from him, and in the process he became famous as well. He travelled about and showed this very, very clever, wise bird.

So that was Belokolodez. But the family estate was called Kamenka; it was eighteen to twenty versts from Belokolodez near Yasnaya Polyana, Tolstoy's estate. My uncle Paul inherited the estate; he was disabled – he had had a stroke, couldn't walk and was in a wheelchair. He had a special troika and a very nice young coachman who had trained those horses to be absolutely still; they wouldn't move until my uncle was safely embarked in the carriage. Uncle Paul lived like a hermit on his estate, with his valet and his coachman and a most marvellous cook, because he liked to eat well. I always remember him sitting at his big writing desk, with candles lit, playing patience. He loved playing patience. He adored me and when I came all my favourite dishes were at once ordered. He gave me my first pony called Zvezdochka. He gave me a most wonderful saddle that he brought from Germany, specially made from suede, some wonderful stirrups and a lovely little stick. He absolutely adored me and spoilt me, and I remember how I could ask for anything.

My strongest childhood memories are of the midnight services and feasts we had to celebrate Easter. In the country we would frequently stay with my aunt Zina at her estate called Malashevo. The house was vast, surrounded by an artificial lake where giant carp used to rise to the surface when a bell was rung. She was married to M. M. Kalita, an aristocrat and descendant of one of the founders of the Russian state. When I was older I was taken to the church services; we used to walk to the church in winter in felt boots called *valenki* and fur coats. Flaming braziers were lit in the church. The picture is fixed in my mind. The congregation, after walking in procession round the church, reaches the altar. The golden gates are flung open and the priest sings 'Christ is Risen.' Then the church lights up and the congregation answers 'Yes, indeed. He is Risen.' Everyone kisses each other three times. I always dreaded this because of all the peasants there with prickly beards. At the house a great feast was waiting for us. We broke our seven week fast with *kulich*, special bread blessed in church, *paskhas*, which are sweet cheese cakes made in special shapes with engraved letters, coloured eggs, roast piglet, and many kinds of vodka and wine. I always remember the wonderful smell of hyacinths, which were grown in profusion in the greenhouses specially for that procession.

We stayed mainly with my mother's relations when I was a child. My father also belonged to the nobility, but not that old Russian nobility, because he came from the south of Russia, from the Ukraine. His name was Sergei Leonidovich Konkevich. There are lots of names like Konkevich there. My father's father was an admiral in the Russian navy – it was he who created the Imperial Black Sea fleet[4] – and that's why they lived in Sevastopol.[5] They lived in a great house on the quay and entertained an awful lot. My grandmother was half Greek, half Russian, and her surname was Potemkin. They had five daughters and two sons. They called their estate Volna which means wave, because of the first names of all the five daughters: Vera, Olga, Lyuba, Nadia and Anya. Then they had two sons, my father and his older brother.

My father read law and then went to Moscow to become a lawyer. He was the assistant of my mother's first husband, whose name was Prilukov, and that's how they met. He became a civil lawyer, but he had very much wanted to be a criminal lawyer because he was a very good orator and he was interested in it. But as he was saddled at once with my mother and two children to bring up, he felt he couldn't afford to do that. Instead he took lots of civil cases, at first small ones, and then he progressed until at last he was earning very well. He represented all the big foreign companies like Kodak, Thornton's, which was a very big English textile firm, Singer and Avanso's Art Store. He had very rich clients, but he always had a sort of *rancune* that he never became what he really wanted to be. His mother never liked my mother, because she thought that she had spoilt his career, and that she had spoilt his life in a way. His personality was very forceful indeed; he was to a certain extent egotistical. My mother was better educated than he was and he often referred to her as soon as there was something more intellectual. He was pragmatic; he was a man of action. He always had an aim; he aimed at it and he did it. I remember my father smartly dressed and smelling of *eau de cologne*, going out either to plead in court or to join his friends in the evening, never with my mother. He used to come in to say goodnight to me and would read some poetry or play a game. Behind the wardrobe we had discovered a cobweb and he used to tell me stories about the old spider who had made it. He had a Chinese name, Lee Hun Gung. My father was always a romantic figure for me, sweeping into my room with his starched white shirt. He led his own life, especially so when he got into the circle of all those rich foreigners. Then he was always off with them for all kinds of amusements. They had a special club, which was called the Konstantinovsky circle. It was a very famous hunting club. They went hunting every weekend with dogs and men who carried all the guns. In summer they used to go fishing. He loved the south where he was born; he loved mountains; he didn't like the flat plains of our family estate in the Tula region.[6] He always said that when he came to stay it made him frightfully sad. It was a sad place; you have to be born there to understand. All those long, long roads, and endless corn fields with big rivers flowing very slowly. He loved the mountains and the riding there. Every summer he went off for a holiday without coming with us. We always moved to Belokolodez, and if he came for a few days we were thrilled to bits. It was really very much his own life. Consequently my mother was on her own a lot, but she wasn't solitary. She was a typical member of the intelligentsia, immersed in her work. In her youth her contemporaries were mostly idealistic, liberal, and convinced that they had to improve the lot of the poor. A great movement started called *khozhdenie v. narod* or 'going to the people'.[7] Young people from rich and privileged backgrounds started schools in the villages as well as evening classes in the towns. My mother was typical of this group. She became a socialist of the Menshevik faction,[8] and was dedicated to workers' education all her life. Her teaching was all voluntary. I never saw her; she always used to go off at six or seven o'clock and didn't come back till late.

She was the head organiser of the Prechistensky Kursy,[9] the Workers' Education Establishment, the first one in Russia. Even the Soviets recognised that – I've got a book about it where they mention her name. Politically she was very much to the left and my father was absolutely uninterested in politics. He wanted to earn well; he was interested to build up his name. It was a quite different approach to life from my mother's.

The flat in Moscow where we lived for quite a long time had seven rooms and that's where my brother Rafa got ill. At 17 a tragedy happened in my brother's life. During the Christmas holidays he went to the country by himself, to Belokolodez for a day or two of shooting. He was very fond of hunting and we had a lot of dogs specially kept for hunting; they had a little wooden house like a big kennel where they all lived together. Well, after a long day's shooting he came back exhausted to the bailiff's house for dinner. It was a good dinner, and Rafa had a few glasses of *pertsovka*, which means pepper vodka; it's brewed with pepper and it's very strong. Rafa went to bed but in the middle of the night he woke up hot and very thirsty, so foolishly, and not being used to alcohol, he rushed out and rolled himself in the frozen snow. He ate some of it, and went back to bed in all his wet clothes. The result was a severe cold. He arrived back in Moscow and went straight to bed. We had all been invited to Anya's christening, the youngest daughter of my aunt Zina. Naturally Rafa was left at home in bed. Suddenly during our feast the telephone rang and one of the maids who had been left at home said that after a fit of coughing, Rafa had begun to spit blood, and had just had a haemorrhage. My mother rushed back home. The doctors found that my brother had an acute pneumonia and one of his lungs had been touched so tuberculosis had developed.

There was great upheaval in the house. He was moved to my big nursery as it was the best room in the house.

My mother was terrified that he might be contagious and decided that I must move from the house. I, together with Doylia, went to live with some friends. They were quite well off as they kept horses and a coachman which was a sign that they were rich. Originally they came from the Baltic provinces, so their name – Riddle – is of German origin, although they were Russian. I was brought up in a very liberal atmosphere; both my mother and my father belonged to the Russian intelligentsia and they had all its liberal traditions. When we moved to the Riddles', I had the feeling that we were moving into another world. I think that they were really still serf exploiters and proprietors. It was 1915 but they still had all that in them. To me it seemed a dark world, a forbidding world. The family consisted of an elderly brother Sergei Fedorovich, his sister Maria Fedorovna, and four children: Serega, Lyolia, Kolia and Liza. Sergei was the children's father, but their mother, who was not married to him, was a simple peasant woman who lived on their estate in the Novgorod region.[10] They lived in Moscow during the winter. They had carriages, horses and coachmen, a butler and a cook and were far better off than us. They came from the nobility. The poor peasant mother wasn't allowed to be with her children. She couldn't live with them in Moscow and was only allowed to come and see them at Christmas and Easter. She used to come in her peasant clothes, in a large shawl and bringing whatever she had, sweets or something for the children. She sat in the chamber hall on a little chair and that's where the children came to see her. Sergei Fedorovich never saw her, and Maria only allowed her to see the children for half an hour or so. Otherwise these poor children were entirely in the hands of Maria.

Maria had taken them over and decided to educate them and bring them up herself. Sergei was in a wheelchair, paralysed from the waist down. Maria was a real tyrant; she was always dressed in black. I still remember her vividly: grey hair, a wrinkled face, small peering evil little eyes. The servants and children all feared her. She whipped them mercilessly with a bunch of twigs brought in from the garden. They were brought up in a very severe fashion. To me this was incomprehensible because I had never seen or experienced any sort of punishment like that. The big grim house, the retinue of servants, the whole atmosphere seemed awful to me.

I don't know what happened to the rest of the family during the Revolution, I only know that Lyolia became a prostitute. She used to go and hunt in the boulevards and bring back clients to the dingy basement of the big house where she now lived with Maria. They say Lyolia used to beat this Maria whom she had hated since her childhood, and I always thought it was a good retribution.

Doylia and I stayed with the family for about two months until my brother was well enough to travel to the Crimea to recuperate. Doylia's job at that time was at the school where she had a job as a class madam. In Russia every class had a person, generally a woman, who used to supervise the children. She sat in on all the lessons, to see that they listened to the teacher and worked hard. She used to go there from about nine o'clock in the morning until four in the afternoon. While Doylia was away I had a French governess to look after me; we had a very good time. My mother found out that our walks together would very often end up in a French confectionary shop. In the basement of this shop there was a bakery which made wonderful cakes. This Mademoiselle Corbeau, my governess, had a lover there, and she always used to take me which I enjoyed because of all the sweets.

My mother went to the Crimea with my brother and stayed somewhere near Yalta. My aunt was commissioned to take me there and these preparations for the journey I remember so well, as I was so excited to be going south. I remember that I had a special coat made of white wool and a white hat with flowers on it. I felt so excited and so smart. We arrived at the station, got a porter and were escorted to the carriage. We had to wait quite a long time as our father was meant to come to the station to say goodbye and bring our papers and money and so on, but Tetya Masha was a bit worried because he was late. It was a very comfortable carriage with a lavatory inside it. That journey was wonderful. We made friends with some people in the next door carriage. They were husband and wife with a young boy of my age. We had a lovely time running and playing along the corridor of the train, and going to have our meals in the restaurant car. The conductor who sat with the samovar used to bring me hot milk even at night. The whole day passed in an excitement, and then in the evening we went to bed. I was in the top shelf and Tetya Masha was one below in the bottom shelf. I remember well that I woke up very early next morning and opened a curtain and suddenly I saw an absolutely wonderful sight. We had come from Moscow and it was still very cold with snow and everything, and suddenly we were in the most wonderful place with magnolia trees blooming and bright flowers on the ground.

At last we arrived in Simferopol, which was the last station on the way to the Crimea. In Simferopol we were meant to change to a car. There were cars with four or sometimes six seats which went round the mountain to Sevastopol. This was the most beautiful road; it wound around and on one side there were the most lovely parks and villas. On the other side there was the sea. Tetya Masha got frightfully annoyed because our other companion in the car was an elderly man who had a terrible cough and an awful cold. Tetya Masha was afraid that I should catch a cold and she tried to open the windows the whole time, and he said 'You mustn't open the windows because there's too much draught.' They argued all the way there.

Then I began to feel sick, because of this steep downwards path. I was sick out of the window, and at last we arrived in Sevastopol, and we were met by my aunt Olga and my cousin Vera. We all got into a horse-drawn carriage, and went to a big house which stood on the quay. This house had belonged to my grandfather. Then we all came out on to the terrace and looked at Sevastopol. It was so pretty under that sun because most houses there were white and shining, and we could see the sea.

What about your political memories?

One of my strongest memories is of the 1914 declaration of the First World War. At that time we were at our estate Belokolodez and my brother used to get the post every morning. The post was three or four miles away from the estate, where the administrative buildings were. He used to go in the morning, riding on his horse. He came riding poste haste back and said 'You know that war has been declared between Russia and Germany.' We all got into our carriage and went to see what was happening. When we got there, lots and lots of peasants in their carts were already being called up. A clerk sat inside putting down all the names of the men and the horses. All the women came to say goodbye. They were crying and sobbing and saying goodbye to their husbands, sons, fathers, etc. It was a lovely bright morning. It was the 14 July.

When I was bigger I remember that first morning after Rasputin was drowned. All the papers were full of it. Everyone was saying that one of his galoshes had been found under the ice of the River Neva in St Petersburg. I also have a great impression of the first Revolution, when the Provisional Government was in.[11] Everyone came out into the street, and there was such jubilation. I was quite a young girl then, about 14 or 15. Everyone was in the streets. There was such joy at the Revolution and the government – they all felt that Russia was ready for a democratic government.

As far as I remember, my life as a young child, and my parents' life, didn't change very much between the two Revolutions, between March and October, the Provisional Government and the October Revolution. That first summer as usual we went to Belokolodez, but there were already a lot of changes in the countryside. My mother decided that she was going to invite another family to share the house with us; she wasn't very practical. Anyway, she got hold of a family who were the Rebinkins. The father was working in some kind of ministry, and his wife was one of those so-called intellectuals who was working with my mother. They had a little boy and a grandmother. They all descended on us at Belokolodez thinking that they would have a very nice few months' rest in the countryside. Everyone was furious with my mother – they just did not fit in.

First of all, the grandmother only had one arm; I don't know why, but she lost one arm in some kind of accident. She loved playing *gorodki*, a game very much like croquet, and she managed to play with one arm, but she always exasperated us. Whenever we wanted to play, she was there in our way, and we used to hate it. And they didn't bring any food with them and kept on eating all our food. Doylia and Tetya Masha were furious with my mother. Then all kinds of unrest started in the countryside; the peasants used to come in hordes, and demand this and that, and the Rebinkins got awfully frightened. My mother wasn't a bit frightened, but they were scared.

We all had to start working, because there was no more hired labour and there were no servants, so we had to do everything ourselves. Those silly people did nothing except eat our food. My little French governess, Mademoiselle Corbeau, was very good. She was so energetic, she used to wear a little short skirt and boots, and was always ready to help with everything. She used to clean the stables, brush the horses, and do all kinds of work. She carried a big *nagayka*; it's a sort of whip made out of leather to scare all the little boys who came to steal our apples. She used to run after those boys. She had only a few words of Russian, all swear words. She always wore those high heels; she was a marvellous character. She came from Rennes, and she lived with us in Moscow as well as Belokolodez. The Rebinkins left, and we had to leave very soon after that because it was starting to be frightfully unpleasant. The Soviets wanted to take our house away. My father said 'You must come back to Moscow', so we left, went back to Moscow, and we never saw Belokolodez again.

At once all the flats were confiscated and made communal, and other families put in them. Of course my father was very clever; he thought of it all beforehand. He managed to get two families to share our flat, but luckily it was very big, so it wasn't too bad. We had two rooms, and the others all had two rooms. We got Baltisky who was a general in the Soviet army. He used to be a general in the Tsarist army, but he went off to the Red army. Baltisky's wife and two daughters occupied one part of the flat, we had the other part, and the last part was occupied by Nekora who was a civil servant. The Nekoras had two grown up daughters who were typists or clerks in some office or other. They had been expelled from their own place when it was taken over by the authorities. Those Nekoras were always frightfully hungry and they somehow never managed to get any food. Their rations were taken away and they were in a very bad way. But the Baltiskys had a lot of food because he got lots of supplementary food rations from being in the Red army.

Our cook and our maid still remained, and lived in the flat with us. The cook still cooked for us, and she always used to steal everything from that Baltisky. I was always so hungry you know, at 16 and no food, so she used to pinch something from the Baltiskys' so always I had something when I came home from school. Masha, our former maid at Belokolodez, was a very devoted girl. She got married in the village and then she managed to visit us in Moscow. They all knew that we were so frightfully hungry in the towns and she used to come and bring us all kinds of things like frozen potatoes. Even frozen potatoes at that time seemed a luxury. So we lived all right and I remember my birthday was celebrated. I must have been 16 and so I asked all my friends. Of course there was no food, but our cook managed to do something, she made some lovely little cakes out of potato peelings. She sweetened them with saccharin, and made something else with cod-liver oil. My father somehow managed to save a few lumps of sugar, and he had an enormous pincer that he used. Every lump of sugar had to be cut into small bits and dipped into the tea with the pincer. It was so wonderful to drink tea made with carrots. We used to drink carrot tea with those little lumps of sugar.

The rations that we got were terrible; the bread was very bad. For some reason there was always straw inside with the husks from the wheat. Well that's how we lived, but of course I was young, and thought it was wonderful. I remember my father once gave us a lot of his old ties. He had quite a lot of ties because in the old days he used to dress up. I went with my friend to the open market and stood there selling those ties and then we had just enough money to go and buy ourselves a little round, white bun, one each.

I was at a private school, which after the Revolution was taken over by the state and made co-educational. Oh we loved it. We managed the school ourselves, and we had the boys there. It was such an interesting time. We in the upper forms organised the whole of the curriculum; the school life was in our hands. The teachers only taught. This happened after the first Revolution; the idea was to put everything into the hands of the pupils so that they should organise their own school life. We used to invite all the artists from the theatres in Moscow to give us talks and perform in the school. We organised all kinds of clubs, dancing circles and singing circles. We produced lots of plays. All the private exhibitions opened, and in the same street as our school, which is now called Kropotkin Street, there was the famous Impressionist collection of two Russian merchants. We used to go there for hours from school to look at those masterpieces.

We also had to manage to feed the school. We organised different meeting points in different parts of the town where you had to go and fetch the food, and bring it back to all the schools. We used to go with enormous churns to all those communal kitchens to bring back soup. Awful soup it was with herring bones and herring heads. We had our little ration of bread; it was just a tiny bit. So we were very busy. Instead of working at our studies we spent a lot of time doing all that. But it was fun; you know in youth everything is fun. We had big sledges and we used to fetch all the provisions. We really enjoyed ourselves. We went to every imaginable theatre and cinema because we had free tickets to go anywhere. Everything was free – all the private exhibitions. They were wonderful, those summer months before the October Revolution. My main recollections of Moscow were that everywhere there were meetings, on every corner someone was talking. Everyone ate lots of sunflower seeds the whole time, so all the pavements were covered with sunflower seeds and husks. Everyone was talking, talking, talking, and there was always a meeting of the representative of the traditional government talking about how we must be faithful to our allies, and that we must continue with the war and wait for the constitutional assembly. We would have a democratic government, but first of all we must finish the war because we've got our allies and we've promised them this and that, and otherwise we will lose to the Germans.

During the October Revolution,[12] we had to move out of our flat and live on the staircase to be safe from the gun fire. It was interesting to live under the staircase; all the mattresses and pillows were put out. There was a very famous singer Dobrovolskaya who lived in one of the flats, and she not only got out her mattress to sleep on, but also her piano because she wanted to practise her singing. It was lovely for us to be able to hear her.

Once I was looking out of the window and suddenly I saw a hand come out of a nearby chimney-stack with a gun. Someone else was crossing the road and the hand was trying to shoot him from that chimney-stack. My brother, who was on the Tsarists' side, managed to get to us for an hour or so, to sit and have some food or a rest from the fighting. He came several times; of course it was dangerous, but there you are. But that first morning after the Revolution, when the Bolsheviks took over, I remember so well. It was a beautiful sparkling day and there was peace and quiet. Then I looked out of the window and saw that the Red soldiers and patrols were standing there, just outside the Kremlin gates. Our house was just opposite, and all the White officers, all the boys of our acquaintance, everyone was filing through. They had to throw away all their ammunition, so there were piles of ammunition lying on both sides. They went through a chain of Red Guards wearing leather jackets. Many of them were Estonians, and they stood on both sides. They were the police of the time and were supervising all these young people throwing away their weapons. Then the White soldiers were taken prisoner and led away as soon as they discarded their revolvers and their guns.

My mother wanted to know where my brother was, because we

had heard nothing. So she dressed up in old clothes and a big shawl and went round the bars and streets looking at all these dead bodies lying about, wondering if perhaps she'll find him. But she didn't find him, and came home frightfully distressed. Three days later a friend of his suddenly arrived and told us that Rafa was all right; he was hiding somewhere outside Moscow. He was hiding and moving from place to place.

Next somebody came to search us because the porter downstairs told the authorities that we had a White officer who used to come to our flat. They put a warrant into my father's hand and he had to lead them all through the house; they searched everything. They found nothing, but a few days later they came and arrested him. They found out that he had been a lawyer to all those big foreign firms and on those grounds he was arrested. They were his clients and friends at the same time, all foreigners, and that was very suspicious. The regime wasn't as severe as it was later in Stalin's time, because he even took a volume of Shakespeare with him to prison. I've still got that book with his markings made while he was sitting in that prison and what he read at that time. He loved Shakespeare; he knew it so well and would recite it always. The marks used to say that he'd read these lines on such and such a day in Butyrki prison just after an interrogation.

After two months my father came out of prison, but it was very difficult to find any sort of job for him, because he was a lawyer and at that time they didn't employ lawyers anywhere. He couldn't get a job, and so for quite a long time there was nothing.

My father finally managed to get a job in a cooperative. There were one or two old cooperatives left in Moscow, and they were taken over by the state. He managed to get a job as a lawyer there. After some time they wanted him to go abroad, to England, and he was assigned to go there. He thought it was a wonderful opportunity. The cooperative he worked for was keen to start a trading relationship with the West. At that time they weren't regulated so much by the state; there was a certain freedom. He managed to take us with him because the people who directed it were as yet not the real government watchdogs. My mother was not keen to leave Russia, but of course as she didn't know where her son was, and she wanted so much to find out what had happened to him, she agreed to go. Rafa had escaped from Russia, but we didn't know where he was.

It was a frightfully difficult journey for us to get out of even

Moscow. All the trains were so crowded, there were no ordinary passenger trains, there were only what they called *teplushki*. That's a sort of cattle wagon. You had to get into these trucks and I think we were at least twenty-four hours in the station, sitting there trying to get into one of those *teplushki*. My father was a very strong man; he was dressed in a peasant coat and had grown a beard on purpose before we left to look very wild and very strong and peasant-like. We were covered in shawls, and somehow he managed to push us into one of those *teplushki*. It was a most stressful journey; I think it took us at least four days to travel that comparatively short distance from Moscow to Minsk and there was no lavatory. Luckily at this time we all wore long skirts. My mother had a kettle with her, so we used to push it under our skirts, use it as a chamber pot and pass it on to the lucky ones by the window to empty. Our aim was to get into Poland.

When we finally got to Minsk it was late at night but we managed to get an *izvozchik* (a cab) which took us to some shabby hotel. They gave us a room in which there was one enormous double bed which was crawling with all kinds of insects, so that night we slept on the floor, covering it with a rug that my mother had in one of the sacks. From Minsk we got to another place, Gomel.[13] Here we spent three months. Gomel was a town within the *cherta osediosti*,[14] that was an area in which Jews were compelled to live during Tsarist times. My father thought Gomel would be a good place to stop our journey. He thought that eventually the Poles would get there, that they would take it, and then we would be on the other side of the frontier. So we waited and spent the whole summer there. There was a lovely old garden, with lots of apples and berries, so altogether it was a very beautiful place. There was a very big castle belonging to a Pole, with a beautiful garden and house. That was already taken over by the Bolsheviks, so it was in rather a dilapidated state, but it was still very picturesque. My father looked after a White officer who had escaped from the Red army and who was hiding somewhere in the garden. He lived there for a few weeks and my father fed him; every night he used to go out with some food for him. But he never told anyone, although I think my mother knew, because of course it was frightfully dangerous.

My mother brought some rings and some precious stones out of Moscow, and a milliner made some cherries out of red wax as an ornament for a hat that my mother had, and inside each cherry there was a ring; how she did that I don't know. When we got abroad to Warsaw we needed some money, and that's what we lived on – those stones. So that I remember distinctly. My father dressed in kaftans, and I remember that I had a skirt that I absolutely adored. All our luggage consisted of two sacks with a few underclothes stored in it, as well as my mother's hat. We had shawls over our heads.

At Gomel we waited and waited and then my father found out from someone that it would be much better to move to a little place called Mozyr. He found some man whose name was called Levin. He was a Jew who specialised in smuggling people out of Russia. My father paid him and he said the first step would be to move us to that other town. He arranged for us to stay in a flat in a house belonging to a Jewish dentist. The dentist had died but his wife was still there. She was a very fat woman; I remember her very well – she was always cooking in the kitchen. It all smelt dreadful, all kinds of fried onions.

We were given a little room where we all stayed together. Next door to us some Red army soldiers were billeted, whose pastime in the daytime was to lie on their beds and outswear each other. They swore, they invented all kinds of swear words, and they lay there all day long because they had nothing else to do. They were on a patrol. My mother was always so afraid that I should learn all those awful words, and she kept on saying 'Don't listen,' but you couldn't help but listen. They had another game which they loved; they used to spit. They put a target on the wall in their room and they tried to see who could outspit each other. Absolutely impossible things I remember really, but it had such an impression on me as a young girl.

We must have been there for about a week, and then Levin said 'Well now it's time to go.' He told us how to dress to make ourselves look very inconspicuous. My father borrowed a shawl from that fat woman and she wouldn't give any other shawl but the one that she always wore round her belly while she was cooking. It was an awful shawl, dirty and smelling of those onions, and my father made me put that on my head. I remember the main thing that occupied me was not to have that shawl over my face or my lips, but my father kept pulling it round my head. He didn't want all the soldiers to look at me; I was young and pretty, and he was afraid somebody would notice me too much.

We travelled part of the way in a train; then we stopped

somewhere and Levin said 'We have to change to sledges.' We changed on to a big sledge and there were some other people. He had groups, so we weren't the only family. We were all put in that sledge late at night, and we had to cross the frontier during the night. It was the most marvellous journey to me because it was so mysterious. We went through the woods, and there was snow, and Levin kept on saying 'Be silent, be silent, you must not talk.' Suddenly he would stop the horse and say 'Stop, be quiet, be quiet,' because he knew that the patrols would be crossing the road at a certain time. Then we went on and at last he said we would stop for a few hours. We got out of the sledges, a door was opened into a hut and we went in. I had never seen such handsome people; they were sitting round a fire. Young men and women who struck me as absolutely out of a fairy tale they were so handsome. They were some kind of Jews that lived there, on the frontier. We had to stop a few hours, because they knew when the patrols were going to move. We stayed in that hut, and I always think of those wonderful, beautiful faces. If someone had made a film of that, it would have been marvellous. Towards morning he said 'Well, it's time to go out.' And then we went on, and we got through the frontier.

There were lots of people who didn't get through, who were killed, who were shot. But Levin was very clever. I heard afterwards that he was caught in the end. We came to a small place where the Polish frontier guards were. As there were a lot of refugees the Poles didn't let us through; we all had to be imprisoned at once. The Poles were afraid of spies, and so the women were separated from the men and we were sent to prison. My mother and I were with some other women and children; my father was with the men. We stayed quite a long time and got very meagre rations but I got a great admirer there. I've forgotten his name now, one of those Polish soldiers.

We stayed in the prison for quite a long time, and they interrogated everyone. They asked my father whether anyone could vouch for him, and my father mentioned a Polish cousin. When he mentioned this name, the guards got very interested and said 'Well you know he is a hero now? He was in the war; he became a general; he is a hero.' They sent a telegram to him at once, and he answered back and said of course he knew us, and so we were put into a diplomatic train. At that time of course we had awful clothes and only had sacks with us. Suddenly we were in that diplomatic train with generals all in wonderful uniforms and medals. I felt absolutely dreadful. There was even a wagon restaurant there where we could eat, with waiters. Suddenly such luxury after all that misery in the camp where we had slept on wooden planks. That's how we got to Warsaw.

Warsaw at that time, in 1920, was absolutely wonderful. All the armies were there: the French, the British, the Americans, the Czechoslovakians. It was so brilliant, full of restaurants and cafés. Warsaw seemed beautiful to me. It was winter and we lived in the Allée Rouge, the Rose Avenue, and the name seemed so romantic. Our friends took us in, and we stayed in their house. It was all very luxurious and we were so shabby, so poor and everything. They gave some clothes to my mother and I had something.

My father started trying to arrange to go on, because his aim was to get to London; his papers were for London. We stayed there about a fortnight and then we got to Paris, and Paris seemed lovely. It was already spring, the chestnuts were all in bloom, and they were selling roasted chestnuts in the street. My father got a guide for my mother and myself because he was very busy; he had to go to all kinds of ministries. An old man took us all over Paris. We were staying in a little hotel with a big glass window and trees outside.

At last we made the journey to London. We got to London and it was already late autumn. It was cold and it was grey and it was awful. We got to Victoria by train and stopped in a little hotel. It was so cold and there was still rationing in England, so that there was no heating whatsoever. It seemed awful after those two big, wonderful cities that I had seen.

My first memory is that everywhere near Victoria station there were big horses with wagons. There were no cars then; everything was transported by horses. I didn't like London; I hated it. From that little hotel in Victoria, we moved to another in the Aldwych, the Waldorf Hotel. It is quite a good hotel, but the windows were broken and it was so cold in the room. The first night I went downstairs with my mother; my father was never there – he was arranging all his business. There were just the two of us, and we went downstairs to have some dinner, and were frightfully surprised when we got to the dining room – everyone was in evening dress. You know, English people even then dressed for dinner. Then we went to the theatre – we didn't understand very much, but we still went to the theatre. The first play that we saw at the Aldwych Theatre was called *Tea for Two*. My father went with us, and he of course knew English quite well, so he explained more or less what went on. My mother and I went round London, trying to see all the sights.

LUDMILA MATHIAS

Ludmila Mathias was born in St Petersburg on 19 September 1905. She was the daughter of Leonid Krassin, who became Commissar for Foreign Trade under Lenin. They lived in London and Paris for six years, but were shunned by the majority of people in the West for being the family of a Bolshevik diplomat. She married the barrister, civil servant and documentary film maker John Mathias in 1931, was widowed in 1963 and now lives in London.

My very first memory was so joyful and happy. I was on a very narrow path walking through tall green grasses on either side of me. I must have been very small because this green forest was taller than my head and the effect of the sun shining through the tall grasses was very beautiful and made me feel happy. We lived in Moscow and Leningrad, and Tsarskoe Selo.[1] My first memories of my father were in Germany, that was in 1908 or so. I was about 3 then. My father had an apartment in Berlin; we all came there after my mother had given birth to my youngest sister while she was still in Russia. Once that had happened, she took all three of us and we went to Berlin. When we arrived in Berlin my first memory of my father was walking along the station; I was holding my father's hand, and in the other hand he was carrying a hat box, which was square in shape. The baby – my youngest sister Louba – was in that hat box. We always teased her: 'Oh, you arrived in Germany in a hat box.'

Father[2] was exiled in Germany after he got out of prison in Finland – he had been imprisoned for revolutionary activity. Some incriminating papers had been found in Finland – where we had our dacha house for holidays. He was imprisoned by the Tsarist police of Finland, because Finland was part of Russia at the time.[3] He knew Lenin as a student; he was a student at the same time. These revolutionaries were persecuted then, and many of them were exiled. Father had joined the Bolsheviks to work with them. You know how the students in Paris had a Revolution (1968), well, it was like that in Russia. And they were studying Marx; little circles got together to discuss Marx. My father was a member of one of these circles – there he met Lenin. He was critical of Lenin, and didn't agree with his ideas before the Revolution, and he was very sceptical when the Bolsheviks got into power. This he told my mother in his letters; he didn't believe they would succeed.

When he escaped from Finland, from prison, he went to Berlin to get out of Russia and worked for three years with Siemans Schuckert,[4] he was a very talented engineer. He built the power station in Baku before the Revolution; it is still functioning now. Another of his engineering achievements was the electrification of part of Petersburg. He had some quite high, influential friends in Russia and returned three years later; there was some work to be done and Siemans Schuckert had made him their Russian representative. You see he wasn't worried about getting into trouble with the authorities because he'd had some very important jobs to do. I think he was in charge of some very big industrial and engineering jobs. Finally, during the 1914 war, he was the managing director of two armaments factories, two big enterprises. By that time all his past revolutionary activity had been given up. He had started making money in Germany and he did very well in Russia as he was at the head of three big firms. He was an industrialist, not interested in gains for himself, but anxious to provide for his family and a perfectionist in his work and engineering which was his great interest.

I have seen the house in Tsarskoe Selo where we lived, it is now made into offices for the municipality. There are two palaces at Tsarskoe Selo, and a lovely park where we went walking every day with our beloved French governess. In summer we went to the country near St Petersburg, in a dacha with a huge garden. These were very happy summers. And there were always lots of people. My mother was very hospitable; she had many friends, relations – there were the governesses and the tutor. So we were a large family, and I remember once in Finland where we went one summer she had to take two dachas because one wasn't big enough. And it was a very happy family life.

During the First World War, we carried on as usual. I remember my mother made me knit a scarf, which I did very badly, for wounded soldiers. At one of my father's industrial enterprises they had a whole hospital, and she used to visit it. She told the story of how she came to meet the train that was bringing back the wounded. She said there was a man who had lost both legs, just the trunk left and two arms, as he was wheeled along, he said to her 'How wonderful life is.' She nearly collapsed with horror and pity. So she dragged us to these hospitals once or twice, and me bringing my awful scarf.

I remember my cousin Ninochka aged 15. After an illness, her heart was badly affected. The poor girl was obliged to take great care, to rest, never to run, she spent a lot of time indoors, playing the piano and drawing. She invented a game which she called 'Hares'. She would draw figures with a hare's head in profile and lovely clothes on the bodies – she was very good at drawing and full of imagination and a great sense of drama. She allocated a family to each of us; she created the whole game. Mine was a poor little officer during the 1914 war. My sister had a general and his difficult, elderly, spoilt wife. Another sister had a colonel whose wife was a terrible flirt, always unfaithful to her husband. Our cousin would tell us what was happening; she did all the talking. And it was fascinating, because it was like a novel. She was a very talented girl; she died very young – she could have been a musician, a painter or a writer. She drew these delicate hare families so well. They were all very smart and terribly aristocratic; they organised wonderful balls, picnics and parties. She was of course influenced by the war, the men hares were all military people. She drew the hares in profile, with their ears down. They wore uniforms, and the ladies long dresses. Maxim Gorky[5] was our neighbour in the country that summer; he heard us in the children's room and listened. Then he came and said 'I like your game; I want to play with you.' We were dismayed; we didn't want a grown up to interfere. 'Draw me a housepainter hare', said Gorky. Ninochka was horrified. What would a common ordinary housepainter do in our smart, aristocratic hare society? But she could not say no to Gorky. So, very annoyed, with a thick pencil she drew roughly a very nasty looking hare, making him as ugly as possible. It was the ruin of our game. Gorky came once or twice. But it was never the same; he had ruined our favourite game. To this day I do not enjoy reading Gorky.

I remember Mayakovsky.[6] First of all one summer as a child, on holiday in Finland, we had a dacha by a lake, with a large garden, a tennis court. Next door was Gorky's dacha, and as he was very friendly with my father and mother, he was very hospitable and used to invite us children to tea. One day we went to tea. There was a round table in the corner of the dining room for the children where we were put; the grown ups were sitting at the long table at the other end of the room. And Mayakovsky sat next to Gorky, a weird looking, tall young man, very black hair, very dark eyes and he had a mauve handkerchief, a scarf in his get-up. He stood up and he began to declaim in a very loud voice, shockingly loud. He used the words 'violet' and 'mauve' often, it seemed most peculiar. He stood and gesticulated, shouting out the words of his poems. It was very odd to us children; we giggled and then burst out laughing loudly. Gorky was terribly angry: 'Get these children out of the room at once.' We were led out in disgrace.

Later I saw Mayakovsky when I was in Moscow in 1924. One evening my mother took me to see friends and a couple she knew. Many Russian Soviet people know that Lilia Brik was a girl-friend of Mayakovsky. She was married and they were all three a *ménage à trois*. I didn't know that at the time. My mother took me to the Briks that evening, I was very shy. Well I had, before coming, acquired a pair of shoes with heels, black shoes with a heel: the first grown up heels, not very high but quite a grown up style. So I was very proud of these shoes; I'd never worn them, but I put them on that evening, for the party. With these shoes and a dress I thought was very pretty, and I thought that I am probably the only girl in Moscow who has a dress like that. Anyway off we went, and at this party there were no young people, only grown ups, no one my age. They were all very intellectual obviously, very witty, intelligent, talking in a lively manner. And I felt frightfully subdued and shy. Mayakovsky was there also, sitting in a chair opposite me, and he stared at me and fixed his eyes on me with disapproval and even contempt. I thought 'I suppose he must think I'm an awful product of capitalism', because I felt that he despised me. And then he said suddenly in a very loud voice so that everyone could hear, 'The price of your shoes is still stuck to the heels.' I wanted to go down through the floor I felt so awful, especially being so shy you know; everybody could hear. So I didn't have a very happy experience of Mayakovsky either. I saw him in Paris once. He was rather in love with a Russian girl there; she later married a Frenchman. And I remember him being rather in love with this girl, and trying to persuade her to go back to Russia with him, but she wouldn't.

In 1917 I remember we were taken to see a ballet in what was then Petrograd. We lived in Tsarskoe Selo, about half an hour from Petrograd, which is like a Russian Windsor, only much nearer to the town. It's a small, charming, provincial town – with two palaces, and a wonderful park. My father went by car every day into his office from there. We were taken to town one day, and we spent the night with some relations of my uncle because we were taken to the ballet, and I remember seeing the streets which were half empty, I remember seeing two dead horses on the streets; that was very strange. The signs on shops were being taken down, because they displayed 'By appointment to his Imperial Majesty', and had the two-headed Imperial eagles on top. 'It's the Revolution,' they said. Katia, my sister, who was eight, did not like it at all 'I was going to be the grandest hostess in high society. Now there will be no society.'

During Kerensky's Provisional Government in March there was a lot of snow. We went with Mlle Pichon, our French governess, nearly every day to the park where the Catherine Palace is. It has lovely, long avenues, with lots of pavilions, ponds and statues. In this great park before we had seen, two or three times, along these wonderful long avenues, a very smart sleigh – a troika with black horses. In it four girls were laughing, the daughters of the Tsar. The horses were covered with a royal blue net, with huge tassles at the end. They moved so fast, throwing up the snow, and the girls looked so happy, and they were laughing – that was a wonderful sight. That was shortly before the Revolution. Later when the Tsar was deposed[7] and he lived in the Alexander Palace as before, we often passed by there. We could see through the iron railings into the garden of the palace. I remember so well seeing a figure dressed like an ordinary soldier in khaki, shovelling away the snow with a wide wooden shovel, clearing a path. There were two or three other men also in khaki. Mlle Pichon would say 'That's the Tsar,' and I would say 'What's he doing?' 'Oh, he's a prisoner in his own palace, and he's clearing the snow for exercise.' So that's a very, very vivid memory. It seemed a very strange thing for a Tsar to do. 'It's the Revolution,' they said. That was in 1917.

During the Bolshevik Revolution, in October 1917, I was in Sweden, where father sent us during Kerensky's time. Mother took only summer clothes to Sweden, so that we would have to come back in winter. But father said, 'Things are getting worse, and you must stay away this winter' – that was a message through Berlin. He was very sceptical about the Bolsheviks at first and then he sent a message that he had agreed to join their government. He wrote, 'You still have to stay abroad, because maybe this is not going to last, maybe I will have to escape, and I would be so worried about you.' After that he visited us twice for a short time, before the blockade of Petrograd cut us off completely from him.

At that time he was the director of several companies, although everything was falling to pieces. Lenin was terribly keen, having known my father in the past, to get hold of a man like that, because they didn't have so many engineers or able businessmen left after the Revolution. The able people were either exiled, or ran away to Paris, to Stockholm, to Berlin, or they were shot, or sent to Siberia. There were very few left like my father. And so Lenin wanted to get hold of him. It took some time, but he did persuade him finally. Lenin said about him, 'Oh he is like a prima donna, this Krassin – one has to make such a play to get hold of him, to persuade him. It's very, very difficult.' But finally Trotsky helped to persuade him. And my father felt it was rather tempting for him to be able to do something to help Russia in this horrible collapse, caused by the First World War, civil war and the war of Intervention.

There were a lot of Russian émigrés in Sweden by then – they all ran away when the Bolsheviks came to power – and they organised a Russian school for émigré Russians. But they wouldn't accept us, because they knew that father had joined the Bolshevik government. So we couldn't go to school in Sweden. My mother taught us a bit and then we had a French governess who had been with us in Russia and came out with us to Sweden. I had a teacher who came and sometimes taught me to write in Russian, but my mathematics was absolutely zero. I never learnt the multiplication tables; I don't know it to this day, except for the five.

My father was well off, and he had transferred some money to Stockholm for us. We lived quite comfortably and also our nanny came with us. We lived modestly in a flat and there were one or two Swedish socialist friends of my father in touch with my mother. One was a barrister; he had a lovely island and owned a large yacht, and we used to spend holidays there. But we never knew any children, except one boy who lived on this island. We didn't mix with children; we didn't know Swedish. We lived in a small family group – the three of us – knowing one or two children, but we didn't go to school.

We were in Sweden for three years, and then my father was sent to London by the Bolshevik government, where we joined him. No schools accepted us here, except one boarding school, and father said that was no good; he would never see us. He had his Ministry of Foreign Trade in Moscow as well, because he was Minister of Foreign Trade, or Commissar as ministers were called then. He had his diplomatic job as well, so he was so busy always doing one or the other and we would practically never see him. Well-known schools in London wouldn't accept us, except for a progressive King Alfred school, which was absolutely hopeless for me; I learnt nothing. First of all, I knew German very well, I knew French very well and Russian but I didn't know a word of English when I came to England. I was thrust into this progressive school; it was boys and girls, and we had huts instead of rooms in Golders Green, with outdoor passages, just roofed over. The mistresses wore sandals, and had ribbons around their heads, and homespun clothes – you can see the picture. For nine months I sat in the classroom not understanding what was going on – I didn't know what they were talking about. So it took me a few months before I at least began to understand. I had joined the headmaster's Shakespeare reading class. After reading to us he would say 'Put up your hand if you don't understand a word.' And I was always putting up my hand, especially when the word 'whore' came up. And it made everybody laugh, and he would say, 'It's a lady of easy virtue.'

We were very happy children; we were a very close family. I remember my father even more vividly than mother; he was something very special for us. Everyday we had breakfast with him; he had a great sense of humour and wit, and he was intelligent and he had tremendous charm. Even we children felt he was something special. My mother had married three times; my mother was engaged first to father when she was 18 in Petersburg. They got engaged, but they were very poor; they couldn't get married, and he took part in some student demonstration in Petersburg. So he was arrested, sent down from the university, not allowed to live in Petersburg, sent to Siberia. Mother was left alone for her mother died, she had no father, no relations of any kind – but that's another story. She had a scholarship to Lausanne university and she was about 18, so she did the only thing possible; she went to Lausanne. She wanted to be a doctor, but found she couldn't cope at all because when she went into the mortuary to study, to look at the bones, she fainted every time. So she had to give that up. And she decided she would become a dentist, and her aim in life was to look after the teeth of poor Russian peasants. But she never did. In Lausanne she met an elderly professor of Sanskrit – a Russian. He fell for her, and persuaded her to marry him.

We children used to ask her about this, because she loved my father more than anybody else, but she wasn't true to his memory, yes, she married other people. But we understood her loneliness and unhappiness; that is why she married the professor. They lived in Paris, and Lenin, when he was in exile, used to come and visit them. She had a little boy; she called him Vladimir in Lenin's honour. Lenin used to come and visit her and the professor, and sit down at the piano and sing a song in German, a Schubert song about a girl. He was terribly in love with some young Russian student and he was feeling in a very sentimental mood. Can you imagine Lenin singing a love song! But it's true, it's true; I know the melody and I know the words of the song, because my mother told me: 'You have silks and satins and beautiful eyes – what more do you want?'

> Du hast Diamanten und Perlen
> Und Sammett und Seide so viel,
> Du hast ein Paar blauer Augen,
> Mein Liebchen was willst Du noch mehr?

Then my mother and her husband went back to Russia; he was professor of Sanskrit in Tallinn in Estonia. Estonia was part of Russia then; mother and her husband lived there a few years. We used to say to her, 'We can understand the first one, but why did you marry the second?' 'Ah', she said, 'he walked for one year under my windows.' Her second husband was Russian Jewish; he was a barrister. He was baptised so it was possible for him to live in Petersburg. He was very interested in the theatre and he used to write children's books; he formed an amateur theatrical society and persuaded mother to join it. She was delighted, she said, because she was so very bored, very young, and longing to go out and enjoy herself. She would ask the professor 'Let's go out and do something Dmitri.' And then he would say 'But where can we go?' and went back to his books. So she had rather a dull time with him in a provincial town. And then the barrister appeared, and set up the theatre and went round begging her to perform in a play. That way her other romance started, and she had two children. Ten years afterwards, when she was 28, my father appeared again. She had to give everything and be with him, because he was the true love of her life, very romantic. So we were a complicated family. Her two younger children stayed with their father for a bit, except for holidays; they always joined us for holidays. Later they stayed mostly with us, and they loved my father as much as their own. They adored him.

You could get out of Russia perfectly easily in the very early days of the Bolsheviks. This business of stopping came later, so everyone could get out if they had the means. When my father came back to London for the second time it was as chargé d'affaires. By that time he was less critical, and loyal to Lenin, because he was so anxious to help put the country back on its feet. He hated Stalin, whose career was just beginning. My mother always repeated this to me. A lot of people in Moscow and Leningrad – when Lenin died – said that it would be a good idea if my father succeeded him. But my father was never ambitious for political power; he didn't want political power at any time. His aim was the practical business – industry, reconstruction, factories, trade and putting Russia on its feet again.

He didn't have much recognition in Russia during Stalin's day; I saw a Soviet history book for schools – 'Krassin, Leonid' was mentioned, and it said 'A renegade communist'.

In 1923 I went back just for a few months for the first time and saw all the propaganda, Lenin's portraits everywhere. Placards with communist slogans stretched across streets, posters or portraits of Soviet leaders everywhere – it looked so ugly to me, depressing. I thought that was awful and it was sad to see how the people lived such a very hard life – shortages of everything. Poor Moscow looked so bedraggled; in the public transport everyone was crowded out, everything was motheaten. A poor, poor country. I was very glad when father was appointed to Paris; I thought how exciting. I could have gone to Oxford, I tried for an exam but I failed. I had an interview with the principal of Oxford who was the head of the women's college, and she asked me 'Do you very much want to come to Oxford?' And if I had said 'Yes', she would have taken me because she was a so-called progressive person, and she was rather curious to have a Russian Bolshevik's daughter, rather rare in those days, in her college. But I said, 'Well really I'd prefer to go to Paris, where my father is now ambassador.' But I was foolish; I would have had a better education and probably a better, fuller life if I had gone to Oxford. But it's foolish to regret it. I might have had a very bad accident, and lost both my legs at Oxford; perhaps it was better like that.

I never saw Lenin. When I went back Moscow that time in 1923, he was already very ill. My father said he would take me to see him one Sunday, but he was so busy that he kept putting it off, and saying 'Oh, we'll go next Sunday.' And then Lenin died.[8] I saw his lying-in-state. That was an extraordinary spectacle; I remember going at night and there were endless queues, dense queues in all the streets near that lovely old building – the eighteenth-century House of the Nobles[9] where he was lying-in-state. There were queues in all the streets leading to it, people were queuing up to go past the lying-in- state. It was at night, there was a lot of snow, so everything was white. It was a terribly cold night, even for Moscow; huge bonfires were lit in all the streets near the queues, so that people shouldn't freeze standing for hours in icy cold. It looked very dramatic because these enormous bonfires lit up the houses and the snow and the queues. Also the black icy sky above made it into a dramatic theatrical décor. Inside the House of the Nobles there were Red army soldiers standing guard. Krupskaya, Lenin's wife, was sitting at the head of the coffin. My mother had told me how Lenin's wife had gone on her knees to Stalin, to beg him not to exhibit Lenin's body in a mausoleum; she said it was against Lenin's ideas. But Stalin wouldn't listen and ignored her request. After my father died there was a rather interesting book published in Russia, reminiscences of various people who had known him. Lenin's wife also wrote an article about him in this collection, saying that Lenin valued him very much and was determined to get hold of him, which he found not very easy, but he finally succeeded. I remember my father saying, when he was asked to be a diplomat, 'Lenin will ask me to be a midwife next; I'm not a diplomat.' In spite of not liking diplomatic work, he was a very good diplomat.

When we first arrived in Britain, father's secretary found us rooms in a small hotel in Hove. We were sent there for a holiday; it was in the summer. Rooms were booked in this comfortable hotel by the sea. It was full of retired army people. They found out who we were because the newspapers were full of Krassin; they knew the name. Three foreign girls who couldn't speak English and they realised we were the daughters of a Bolshevik, Krassin. A delegation of retired colonels approached the manager: 'If these children do not move out of this hotel at once, we will all leave.' The crestfallen manager spoke to the secretary and explained and we went to a small boarding house where nobody cared who we were. There was a lot of publicity about my father at that time; we were photographed in the streets of London too. That was 1921, when we first arrived in England. All this publicity was a bit odd and unpleasant.

My mother was busy organising our home. She received many Russians who worked in Arcos, and had arrived from Russia in this organisation for administering Anglo-Soviet trade. My father organised something called the Moscow bank in London, which still exists, Moscow Narodny bank.[10] He had much to put in order. He also set up Arcos,[11] which had its quarters in a large building in the City; quite a few specialists arrived there from Russia. But poor impoverished Russia had nothing to sell except bristles and timber – much had to be organised. They had to have trade delegations. I remember my father brought with him from Moscow a lot of terribly heavy ingots of platinum instead of money. At first they had no hard currency to pay for what they were going to buy. Then he organised what was called Russian bonds. The Soviet government was obliged to borrow money. A lot of people didn't trust the Bolsheviks of course, so they wouldn't touch the Russian bonds. But some made a lot of money with these bonds.

Three girls in my school had been told not to talk to us by their parents because we were Bolsheviks. We were rejected by many, but not by Ruth Cavendish-Bentinck and her family; they used to call her Red Ruth.[12] Now she was a rather brave soul, and she used to call on my mother at the Soviet embassy, and invite us to tea. And Lady Astor was rather curious; she and Bernard Shaw used to come to visit. My mother had a certain amount of entertaining to do. Some people came, the more intelligent kind, because they were interested in Russia. Lady Astor I remember very well; she asked us to tea with other children at her house which was in Grosvenor Square. We were in the big dining room sitting at tea; suddenly in rushed Lady Astor like a whirlwind. She'd just arrived from Plymouth, and she had to change because she had to go off somewhere else. Her bedroom was next door and she surprised and shocked everyone because she undressed in her bedroom and rushed into the dining room half-naked. Talking to us all the time – I thought it was very peculiar. That's how I remember her. Isadora Duncan also visited us. But I remember Red Ruth, Mrs Cavendish-Bentinck, as rather formidable; she talked to me quite a lot. She was curious I suppose, I don't know, or left-minded, although she wasn't in politics. Some people were interested in us you see. I remember my mother telling me that when George Bernard Shaw came to lunch for the first time, she was sitting next to him. She was trying to make conversation in broken English and told him how impressed she was by English good manners and politeness. 'All crooks are polite' was his answer.

My mother preferred being in Paris to London, where my father went next as ambassador, and where the anti-Soviet attitude was less pronounced. Paris she liked rather well, because the Russian embassy there is a lovely old eighteenth-century house with a large garden, which adjoins the Italian embassy on the other side – it's in the Rue de Grenelle.[13] There were three or four receptions rooms on the first floor, where the walls were covered with silk damask. One was an olive green damask, and there was a red room, and the third one was blue. The White Russian émigrés who'd been living there before us tore all that down, spoilt some of the furniture, and made a bonfire on the parquet floor – all because they were so furious that they had to move out and the Bolsheviks now had the embassy. But they left a very beautiful old table, which was supposed to have been Louis XVI; they left it because it was a museum piece. So that was left undamaged in the ambassador's study; otherwise the furniture was really very badly damaged. My mother had to redecorate the whole place, and she did it very well; she got all the walls covered again before she bought the furniture. She bought antiques. She had a gift for that; she had a great deal of taste.

There was an attempt on my father's life in Paris. As you came in there was a courtyard, then glass French windows and glass French doors which lead into a vestibule. Well, at night always a caretaker was there, for security. One night my mother had a kind of premonition, she was wakened by a noise. She got up, and she went into the vestibule, and she thought she saw somebody moving in the courtyard. And she was very impulsive you know. The guard was asleep in a chair, so she broke the window because the door was locked, and they found a woman in the courtyard with a revolver. She had come to shoot my father, but she was never prosecuted because it was discovered that she was a Russian émigré who was slightly mentally deranged. But it was so extraordinary that my mother thought she had heard something that made her get up in the middle of the night to investigate, although the bedroom was not near.

As a result of the Revolution we lost our country, our roots, our home. Our family was separated and dispersed like so many in Russia. We would certainly have been in danger if we'd been in Russia during Stalin's time, and his ruthless killings. Father disliked him very much, and he never talked about him. He used to talk about Lenin, and mention one or two others in the Russian government, but he never mentioned Stalin. My father wanted to get foreign industrial help for Russia very badly. That was his aim. And he was working on three agreements, three concessions – one was for mining manganese ore in the Caucasus. Another one was the copper mines in the Urals which had belonged, before the Revolution, to Leslie Urquhart, a Scottish engineer whom my father knew well. The third was the Lena gold fields, and I think the concession was given to a Canadian firm. Now he signed these agreements; Lenin gave him more or less *carte blanche*, and Lenin by that time was ill. My father always used to call them 'Those half-wits in the Kremlin', because all those concessions he wanted to contract were stopped or annulled in Moscow. Now whether Stalin had anything to do with it is very possible; I can't guarantee that because I don't know on whom it depended. My father never worked with Stalin; he worked for Chicherin, the Commissar for Foreign Affairs in Moscow. Father had his Ministry of Foreign Trade. Another thing that Stalin did, while father was in Paris, or in London, he appointed somebody – I think Mikoyan – to a post in his Ministry of Trade. So behind his back – it was his method of appointing his own people, and that made my father very furious. When he was ill, father said to my mother, 'I'll never go back to Russia, except with my nose upwards' – when he was dead. He was getting rather fed up I think. He died in London, at work in Chesham House, the Soviet embassy, in 1926.

Leonid Krassin's ashes were taken back to Russia, and now lie inside the Kremlin Wall.

MARIE ALLAN

Marie Allan was born Marie Rettere in Moscow on 25 May 1902. She is a second generation French Muscovite, the daughter of a wealthy coffee merchant. Her father was imprisoned by the Bolsheviks, and the family lived in hiding until they managed to escape to France. She married an engineer, George Allan, in 1925, and they had two daughters and one son. Widowed thirty-two years ago, she now lives with her sister Emilie in London.

Father had thirteen shops in Moscow; his father had introduced coffee to Russia. My father had been in Russia since before I was born, and in 1896 he saw the investiture of the Tsar. He said it was a dreadful thing when the people were going to receive alms from the Tsarevich and the Tsarina. They received shawls, and were standing on wooden stands for his investiture, and they hadn't levelled the floor, so everything fell down, and thousands of people were killed.[1] And so people said, 'It has started in a bad way, and it will finish in a bad way too.' My father saw it; he must have been about 21 or 22. He was terribly shocked, but he was not sitting anywhere – he just went to look. It was dreadful; people were screaming; it was like a disaster, and so many people were being walked on. My father wasn't really in the crowd; he didn't have any reason to receive anything, because he wasn't even Russian. But he belonged to Russian clubs; the mercantile club, to which he used to go in the evening to meet people. He didn't know the aristocracy, but the business people, because the Russian aristocracy, like any other aristocracy, was keeping to themselves; it was natural. Being French on top of it, he was a little bit outspoken in his disrespect.

As children we had a very interesting life in Moscow before the Revolution. So very often children were left by their parents with

83

governesses, but our parents were much more modern in many ways; they took us out, because Moscow was a lovely place. Now and then we were taken to the circus which was the best in the world. And father had a *loge* – a box – always for us. Then we went to the opera – I saw *Eugene Onegin*[2] when I was 14 – and the ballet; in 1910 we saw *The Bluebird*[3] by Maeterlinck. On Sunday the Bolshoi was always at two o'clock in the afternoon for the schools. And the schoolgirls in Russia were obliged to have a brown uniform, and a black pinafore, but if they went out on Sunday, they had to wear white. And the boys of every school always had to stand during the interval; that was in case somebody was sitting in the Imperial box there – a princess or somebody – so all the men had to stand. And you would see little boys standing like in front of a general. But I saw the Tsar only once, in 1913, when it was the 300 years of the Romanovs.[4] The whole family came to Moscow; they went to the big church where they had been crowned. And there was the Emperor and the Empress, and the young crown prince – the Tsarevich.

Except for the one year in 1912 when we were sent to France so that we would speak French between us – we were four daughters – we had always lived in Moscow. To mother we always answered in French, but with father we could speak Russian. We missed Russia very much while we were in France. Because when you are born in a country, you take in the whole atmosphere, for example the Russian cooking; I love Russian cooking. I spent twenty-five years in Egypt; I hate Egyptian cooking, and I will never eat the funny things that people eat now – Chinese, and Indonesian, and Japanese. I hate it. And when we were in the convent, in France, mother and father sent us some Russian black bread, because the black bread is a special thing. You can't understand it until you eat the black bread of Russia, and they sent us caviar. For us, caviar was always on the table; it was like butter, *hors d'oeuvres*. And the poor nuns said 'What is this black stuff?' They used to call it 'shoe polish'. But we liked it, and they would serve it for breakfast. And we used to have hot chocolate and croissants, and they used to serve us the black bread with caviar, with the chocolate. And I said 'I cannot eat it; that does not go.' That was a little misunderstanding, but on the whole they were very nice.

When the First War started in 1914 we were in Germany, staying with some friends in Wiesbaden. My mother was very disturbed because we only had our tickets to proceed to France, and she went to see the bank manager, and he asked her to come to his office. And he said 'Madame Rettere, I am German; we have declared war on Russia. Please take your cash and go. Leave tonight; I believe that it's the last train that will pass to Russia.' And so he was so humane, and he impressed on my mother so much that we must leave this same day, you see, don't wait for tomorrow morning, just leave. So I remember her coming and saying to us *'Mettez vos affaires en valise, nous partons tout à l'heure.'* You know that the trains in Russia were larger than the European tracks, so generally you had to change the train at Brest-Litovsk.[5] And we changed train and boarded another one direct to Moscow. We really arrived with the last train, just in time. And it was extraordinarily kind of that man in the bank; we had been his clients for a fortnight or three weeks, and he lent credit so my mother would not have trouble. He arranged to send a telegram to my father saying 'Your wife is on the last train to reach Moscow.'

Children don't think; their world is their own. We didn't really suffer at the time; we didn't really suffer at all. And the war was like all wars, unpredictable. The first thing which my sister and I remember as being a terrible shock to us was when we went back to school in September and we found that the big recreation space was full of Polish children who had been evacuated. The war started on 28 and 29 July, and the Germans went into Poland, and so all the children had been evacuated with their school to Russia. The Catholic nuns came to the schools which were under Catholic management. Those children had travelled; they were in a dreadful state; they had to be washed and bathed and even clothed. And then we realised that the war was there. These children hadn't seen their parents – their parents had remained in Poland – so that was a tragedy which we felt very much.

In 1915 we travelled via the Volga to Astrakhan,[6] on the Caspian Sea. My father said he would bring us a bit of Russian air. And it was a lovely trip – at that time there was a lull in the fighting; we never heard the cannons and we were far from the complications. The Germans were on one side, and at that time the Russians still had Nikolai Nikolaivich,[7] the great man who was the uncle of the Tsar, and who was in the great command of the army.

We went to Astrakhan, and it was a fortnight's journey from Nizhnii Novgorod to Astrakhan. Nizhnii Novgorod was more than 1,000 years old – the Chinese used to arrive with their tea to trade, and there was a fur market with fur from Siberia. Nizhnii means low; Novgorod means new town. It's a low town. Everything was transported up the Volga. They had very nice steamers, with a very comfortable cabin. Travelling by train or by river in Russia you could see versts and versts – it is not yards in Russia, or miles, it is versts – of beautiful wheat. When we arrived to Astrakhan, and we saw how caviar was prepared and then we came back, also a fortnight. But it was really the only beautiful trip we made during the war.

In July 1918 my father was arrested. Instead of going to our Petrovsky Park[8] dacha, we had been invited to stay with some Russian friends who lived outside Moscow. It was a very big house in the corner of their estate, with white columns and a huge roof. And the dacha had a small house next to it which we rented for the summer. Summer was very short. It started at the end of May, and it was ended by 15 August when autumn started. Our cook was brought there to help, and mother had her maid and we had our little Russian girl who used to help us with our clothes and she used to look after us. We were grown up, but she used to do our hair and prepare our things and bath us. At the end of July one day, we were sitting on the terrace after lunch, and a man turned up, and he had five or six soldiers with him. And he said 'We want to see Monsieur Carlovich Rettere.' He said 'Do you have any arms in the house, because we have to look?' And the maid was standing by and she disappeared; she went to my parents' room and she found my father's two pistols, which means she knew where they were. She took them and hid them in the lavatory; the lavatory was a very old-fashioned one. It was a hole with a basin, and when you flushed it went very low down in the ground and in the autumn when the house was empty, it was cleaned. Well anyhow, she had the presence of mind to put them there. And so they said 'Can you swear you have no arms?' And my father said 'No, I have no arms.'

My father was taken off to Moscow, and it was a very long time before we saw him again. On 15 August we returned to Moscow as well, but we couldn't return to our flat because it had been emptied completely. In the Revolution they can do anything to you. You are interned; they didn't ask 'Would you like to be interned?' They decided that my father was an enemy of the Communist Party. You know, now I speak about it so openly, but for a long time I could only dream about it because it had made such an impression on me. I would scream sometimes at night 'Oh are they coming' or something. I remember being married for at least five years, and my husband would say 'You are dreaming about the Revolution again.' So he used to wake me up, and say stop screaming, you are not in the Revolution now. It's a long time, in the subconscious you see.

In 1918 we were still with our friends. My father was in prison and we couldn't see him. And our father's coffee shops were closed, because father had lots of shops in different parts of Moscow. At the end of August, my sister Emilie went to find out when school was again starting. And she went to the school – in the Lubyanka – and she realised that none of the nuns were there. She went to speak to the headmistress, but instead of a nun sitting there, dressed very simply like a servant, it was a soldier with his leg up on the writing table, quite a youngster, an officer of communism. The man said 'What are you looking for?' 'To find out when this school's starting.' 'Well, this school won't be starting because they have all gone away to France, and this school is now under military guard.' And she said 'Oh, well I can go now that I know school is not starting.' And they said 'Yes well, there are two soldiers with guns who will accompany you.' And they marched her through Moscow, but it wasn't the Moscow she knew. There were many windows broken, the police always standing in the same place, not a single human being. And she found herself on the Grand Lubyanka, which was very near. They stopped at the Cheka[9] – and took her up – and took her into a room to wait. The room had three beds in it for soldiers because they were covered with khaki coats. And she knew that in the Cheka they were killing hundreds of people, because all the time one could hear 'tic, tic, tic' – and it was the machine gun going on. So she looked through the window at the place where she thought it was going on – rather macabre. But then she sat on the bed, and thought 'Well, what will it be? And what will mother say in the evening when I don't reappear.' You know, that comes into your head – she was 15. Suddenly on one of the windows she saw a little light – like the Russians put in front of their icons – lamps with a little wick. Can you imagine, it was in the Cheka, in 1918, and there was a light in front of an image of the Virgin. So as she is a believer, and a Catholic, for her to see a Virgin in the Cheka was colossal. They were closing all the churches then, and because this candle was burning, it meant that somebody lit it every morning and prayed. And she thought 'Everything will go on well for me; in my heart I feel it.'

A man called her and she arrived in a big hall with a big desk, and in front of the desk sat a man of 40, very red, very big, and he was completely drunk. And suddenly out comes a woman – his secretary – who was all in black – military with a tie, she had her hair dressed like a helmet, and big spectacles. And he said 'Why did you come here young girl?' And she explained, but he couldn't understand what she was saying, and he fell upon the table he was so drunk; then he told the woman who was secretary to go away. But they didn't ask her name, which was really amazing, because our father's office was just across the street, and there was written our name – Rettere. So they would have found out she was really a bourgeois, and killed her. But nothing happened. Anyhow it was getting dusk, and they opened a door, and she popped outside into the main street. A soldier told her to go quietly, as if nothing at all had happened.

She had to go home, and it was night, not safe. I think she took a tram, and she went to see an aunt or ours who lived not very far from that Cheka. She went upstairs, but she wasn't very welcome because that aunt of mine had a very young child who she was still nursing, about 6 weeks or 2 months old. The night before my sister came, somebody had shot through the window, and shot my aunt's arm while she was holding the baby, and she had lost her milk in all the paraphenalia. She was in a dreadful state; she had a woman doctor who came to rearrange the dressing, and she was not very pleased to see my sister, and she said 'Go back home because your mother will be worried about you.' So my sister left and came home through the forest; she felt that the forest could not touch her. A few days later my uncle said that he'd found a little flat in Moscow on an inside yard, so there was no opening for us by either window or door on to the main street. We went eventually to stay there, and one felt secure from not having an intruder.

My mother was in a dreadful state and she felt so miserable, but we managed. The furniture was not ours – it must have belonged to somebody else before – and there were two bedrooms, one where my mother and my two little sisters were sleeping, and one for Emilie and I. And mother was frightened that the people who owned the flat would come back. We heard a rumour about my father – that he'd been shot – so I decided to dress up as my mother, and go to the Lubyanka jail. Mother had been to Lubyanka before, and she couldn't speak Russian, and they made fun of her, and they asked her questions which she couldn't even answer. And then I said 'Don't go mother. I can speak and now it's so cold I'll put this shawl over, and no one will know if I am your daughter or if I am my father's wife, because I am grown up.' I was like mother, and I was a very big 15 or 16 years old, rather mature in my face. And I put on that shawl, and I went and had to get permission, had to leave my father's name, and say that he was interned on such and such a date. It was very complicated. I couldn't see my father; they said that he was no longer in prison, that he had been taken to a monastery. And that was easier in some ways, because at least the monastery was not under bars.

Eventually I went there with one of my little sisters. Somebody told us that the commandant of the monastery had a little girl. And my sister, Katherine it was, said to the commandant 'Does your little girl like dolls, because I have one?' And he said 'Well, yes, when you next come to see your father, bring the doll. She may like it.' Which she did, and she was so well dressed the little French doll; I mean you could take her coat off, and put it on, and there were little buttons on her dresses. It was much more interesting that the little dolls you could buy in Russia. And he said 'Oh, what a lovely doll. Well, I think now that every ten days you can bring your father a little food; perhaps he doesn't like Russian food, because he doesn't like very much the food we give him.' So next time we managed to bring him some potatoes, and I don't know what else. Emilie used to go with the other sister to a field of potatoes not very far from where we lived to dig them up. You couldn't buy any meat. On one occasion, my mother bought us some meat, and she was so pleased that she had some food. She said 'It's a very nice leg of lamb.' It wasn't lamb at all; it was a dog. She couldn't eat any at all. I asked her 'Why don't you eat?' She said 'Because I want to leave more for you.' But she had cooked it you see, and well, she couldn't eat it. I ate it because I didn't know; it tasted like bad meat.

Every ten days we used to go and see father. My mother never wanted to go because she was so frightened. I was supposed to be my father's wife, and I was always terrified that my sister would call me by my little name, by my personal name. Everything was on the nerves, and so exhausting. And before that you had to go and look for some food, and stand in a queue the whole night to get some bread. Katherine would start first at seven o'clock; she would stand in the queue, and then Emilie would join her at ten or eleven, and then I, being the eldest one, used to go at two or three in the morning, and then sometimes at six o'clock the van with the bread would arrive. I would take the bread home which was such a blessing – although the bread was not good, but it was better than none. But it's amazing how one can survive on anything. And eventually the winter went by and spring started and we decided that we must go and bring father a little more food. My father was living in a monk's cell with another man. Some of the prisoners used to sleep in wooden coffins, so at least they were warm. And luckily my father had his warm winter coat with him, which he had taken with him to the dacha in July, because he said 'Winter is coming soon.'

My mother secured our tickets to go to France, because we were on the list of the French people who were to be evacuated. And the consul had given us permission, and the passports were stamped and everything. My mother made sure my father's passport was stamped too. My mother said 'You know, we may be leaving this December, but I won't go. You can go with uncle Leo who is going, but I'm not going until my husband is released.' So I said 'What shall we do without him?' And I told my mother, 'I will ask the commandant of the monastery to let father see us to bid us goodbye.' And she said 'Yes, but what if he won't allow it?' And I said 'Well, then we won't go. I mean you don't want to come with us, and you don't want to leave father, so we'll have to wait for another opportunity.' And she said 'Go and speak to him nicely.'

When I went to see the captain of the internment camp to ask if we could say goodbye to father he told me 'I can't give a permit without the permission of Dzerzhinski.' Dzerzhinski was in charge of the foreigners that had been interned. So that's how it was that I went to see Dzerzhinksi. I had never met him before. I said to him 'My father is detained in such and such a monastery.' He said my father was easy to deal with, very obedient and never makes disturbances. 'If he will keep his word of honour that he will return to the monastery I will allow him to spend the last night with you.' I was saying all the time I was my father's wife. I don't think Dzerzhinski believed me. 'You're a very young wife. I know your father's age,' he said. 'Well not that young, just over 20', I said. 'I'd say you were under 20.' Well what could I say, I didn't want to lie? But he was more than sympathetic; I just thought why is such a very nice man involved in all this. I was very naïve. He was good looking but I wasn't at the age where good looks would upset me. My father was dependent on me so I didn't want to say, why are you a Bolshevik? They must have felt they were doing the right thing for their country. I was not frightened. That was in the beginning. After that, he did worse and worse things. He spoke of the bright idea, what we are going to do for the Russian people. I didn't know he was a Pole then, for me he was a Russian.

That same afternoon, 12 December 1918, I arrived at the monastery. And they let me in; I had my pass. And I was so frightened; there was no electricity at all, and I walked up the stairs and they had some huge thick candles which lit my way inside. I walked between those candles on large wooden stairs; every five stairs there was one candle. I arrived on the top; it was huge slabs of stones, flagstones. There was the director's door, and I knocked and he said 'Come in'. And I went in, and it was so terribly dark – he had all sorts of candles on his desk. The light was very dim; it must have been half-past four or five. And he said 'What are you doing here again?' And I said 'Well, this time I come to ask you if you will allow me to take my father to say goodbye to the family.' He said 'And if I say no, what will you say? I said 'Nothing; your will is your decision. I can beg but you don't want it.' He said 'Oh, there is always some ways one can beg to get things.' And I said to myself, well what is he going on about this begging for? And I said 'I'm tired of trying to understand this thing.' And he said 'Are you really your father's wife or his daughter?' And I said 'No, I'm his wife; I'm Marie Rettere.' He said 'You are young.' And I said 'No, I'm not young, I have children.' 'Yes I have a child too, and I know that children don't like to lose their parents.' I was begging him in my heart; I couldn't beg with my mouth. I prayed with my heart to say what will the result be. He realised that I was frightened. You know when you see on pictures, women covered with a shawl keeping their shawl tied round them because they're frightened. It was so cold that night, and he said 'Well, I want you to remember that we are not as bad as you think.' And I said 'I wouldn't have come to see you if I thought that you are bad.' He said 'But you know that I can kill you?' And he took a revolver from his holster and put it on the table. He said, 'You know I can kill you and there will be no trace of you. We didn't kill your husband.' 'No', I said. 'He's a nice man.' He said 'He loves you;

I've talked to him. Now, why does he have to be French. If he'd been Russian he could have been useful to us. French he is of no use. Take him.' So I said 'Thank you, but tomorrow he will be back.'

And then I walked down those steps and I thought I must not lose that paper with his release. And everything was so difficult, and my head didn't work properly. There was a door, and I opened the door, and I said 'Emile Rettere'. And a man got up and said 'Who are you?' I said 'I'm your wife.' And he said 'My wife? How can I know that you are my wife?' And I said 'Well, I have a paper; you can come and say goodbye to us because we are leaving.' 'Where are you going?' 'I don't know; wherever the train will take us.' And then I said 'Well, will you come and say goodbye to the family – your four daughters? The commandant gave me a paper, and you are free for the night to come and say goodbye to us.' And he didn't want to go away really. He said 'You know, I have been here for so many months; I feel here is my home.' And there were about six people with him and they said 'Oh, Carlovich, you have the chance to go.' So he walked; but you know, I had to push him out of the door – he didn't want to move and I said 'Come along, come along'. He was under a funny spell where you can't always see reason. One loses one's intellect when you haven't been eating properly. When we arrived at the main door, I showed my father's pass. And he stopped and read it, and the man said 'Well, prisoner number so and so, you can be here tomorrow when the sun gets up; half-past six.' So father said 'Yes'.

You know, I was so frightened of calling him father, because he'd recognise me. Luckily it was so cold that the shawl was all over me. He didn't think; he couldn't think any more whether I was his wife or not. Running out was a nightmare; he had lost all his willpower. We went out, and I had a piece of paper where his name was written and that he was liberated for the night, and one he gave to the watchman, and other I said 'Where shall I put it?' I was so frightened to lose it. Finally I put it in my mouth, and then I thought, when I talk it will drop out. You decide such stupid things. I had some money on me luckily and I saw a man who was on a sledge, and I took him aside, and asked him 'Will you take me to such and such a place?' I didn't give him the name of the street. I sort of mentioned where he had to take us. He said 'Don't you know where you are going?' I said 'Yes, but as it is a dark night, I will show you where we have to stop.' And off we set. My father was sitting very near me because you are covered with a sort of cloth; his feet are inside with mine, and covered so that the snow doesn't fall on you. And those horses were so miserable that I don't know how they carried on.

And off we went. We were going in the right direction on the highway. It was a big open space and suddenly there were three gun shots. They went so near us that the horse jumped. We arrived and I said 'Now this is a small street; you won't be able to turn down it.' It was a cul-de-sac, and I gave him quite a lot of money; I gave him four gold roubles. I said 'God bless you' and he said 'God bless you too.' And we went out with my father, and he was not quite sure where we were going. When my father arrived on the second floor, he was so tired that he just flopped, and my mother had to get something to eat – he couldn't eat. And she said to us 'Bring me some warm water, and I'll wash his face, and his feet, and I'll dress him.' And his boots she took off, and she gave him a very strong drink with lemon, sugar and she put some cognac in. And he drank two glasses; it was warm on a very cold night, and he fell asleep, and it was the best thing. Next morning, when he woke up he said 'Oh, it is time, I should go.' And my mother said to him 'No, don't go, don't go. Stay with the children otherwise we lose them.' My uncle, who was living in the same house, arrived and said 'Are you all right? All ready?' And we said 'Yes, we were all ready.' We were all dressed up; we hadn't gone to bed. We got to the station, and there we had to wait for quite a long time; eventually we crept in the carriage, a very primitive carriage. They were not for the cattle, but they were very low, third class, everything was hard. We were refugees, and therefore we were on the last train.

We left at about seven or eight o'clock in the morning, took speed, and then about two hours later it stopped, because it had not enough fuel. Father said 'I must be going soon; I promised; I gave my word.' And we didn't want him to talk too much, so my little sister sat on his lap, and talked to her father, and my mother never said a word. She was very brave; she was sitting in a corner too frightened to think. She couldn't speak. And eventually the train went and I asked somebody who was passing 'Where are we?' They said 'We must be on the way to Petrograd. We won't get into Petrograd, but we will go round it and we'll get to Finland.' So the train stopped and we went out, and there was a little sledge, and we put my aunt who had the baby on the sledge. And we passed the frontier. The train couldn't go any further. The border was crossed by hand. And so men in uniform were coming, and we had our passports, and they were prepared for us, and they let us go.

We walked for another five kilometres – which was a long way when you've had no food – and eventually we arrived at a little hut in Finland, and there was food prepared for us. Boiled potatoes, minced meat and tea, sugar and hot coffee. And do you know we ate so much that we all got sick, not from the food, but from being so empty. And my father was the first one to be sick. So I said 'What a pity'. It's not that he couldn't enjoy it. And the little cousin was also sick, and then everyone was. Well anyhow, but then we sat on the train again and off we went to the north of Finland, to two places named Haparanda[10] and Tornio.[11] One is apparently in Norway, and the other is in Sweden. But we took the Swedish one, and went on to Stockholm on a very nice train. In every station there was always food prepared for the needy ones; father drank tea with milk and gradually he got better. We slept very comfortably, and from Stockholm we had to change the train to Bergen in Norway, because we were going to sail from Bergen, and that time it must have by Russian calculations at least into December 1918. In Bergen, the steamer that was coming to fetch us from Newcastle in England couldn't come near because they realised that the harbour was full of mines. So it was useless, and they couldn't keep us in Bergen, so they sent us over to a place called Voss, where we stayed until Christmas. Eventually, we arrived in Newcastle at night, and took a train to London, and then to Paris.

In 1970 I went back to Russia as a tourist. I arrived with a friend who was a little bit in the same situation; her mother was Russian, and her father was French. When we arrived on Interflot,[12] whatever they call the Russian airline, it was in Moscow. I would have done as the Pope does when he goes to a country – I wanted to kneel and kiss the earth. The smell of Russia was something so beautiful that I didn't think of anything else. That smell was something that gave me the greatest joy.

On one occasion I went to the Tretyakov Gallery, and I saw a few pictures owned by my father, because my father was a great connoisseur of art. One thing that really startled me was the bust of Christ with a crown of thorns which we used to have in our dining room. Antokolski – he is really famous; he's like Rodin in France.[13] Anyhow it is lost; you can never have it. It's gone; it's gone. Still, it's nice that what my father has chosen is being still appreciated. It's only people who have something that it can be taken away and lost.

OLGA LAWRENCE

Olga Lawrence was born Olga Schilovsky in St Petersburg in 1914. Her father was an engineer for the Bolsheviks after the Revolution. He and his wife escaped from the Soviet Union in 1922, but were forced to leave their daughters behind, hoping to get them out quickly afterwards. In fact the three girls stayed on in St Petersburg for another year before they escaped. The family were brought to England via Germany by their mother in 1923. Married in 1950 to the art historian, George Lawrence, Olga Lawrence now lives with him outside Bath. They have two daughters and one son. She has another son by a previous marriage.

I was born in St Petersburg in 1914. My parents were really rather grand – my father was a provincial governor, and my mother was the daughter of a provincial governor, and she was lady-in-waiting at the court. So it was – so to speak – a very poor insurance risk when the Revolution happened.

I have the haziest memories of the Revolution because I was 3 then – I was tiny. We went down into a cellar. I thought it was really wonderful, but as a child I could have been killed. I just remember everyone being unaccountably frightened and worried and snappy, and fairly unlike the solid grown ups that one had known. Everything was just suddenly different, and you realised that grown people could in fact be frightened. Not the usual sort of Olympian characters. You see the Revolution came at the end of the summer, when everyone was on their estates in the Crimea and the Caucasus and down south. We in fact didn't have any estates or splendid houses like that; most of our stuff was in the centre or the north. So we were sitting there, but my grandfather was out in the Crimea with my cousins.

My father, apart from being a provincial governor, was in fact a scientist – a physicist. And if things had been totally different, he would have been a really considerable scientist – he got a college silver medal. He didn't get the gold medal because of his really 'shocking' behaviour – he used to cut classes. But I mean, brain-wise, he was extremely able, so actually he even got a job in the Ministry of Reconstruction after the Revolution because they'd killed so many of the intelligentsia. You see they had to reconstruct the country, and eventually they needed people. He didn't direct gangs of labourers, but he worked from an office for a time, but it was very, very shaky. I mean, they were liquidating people. Nobody stood a chance if they discovered that they had a privileged past – however good and however useful – out you would be. So in 1922 – we lived in Petersburg then – we managed not to be turned out of our flat. We were country people basically, and lived on our modest estates – we only had a flat in Petersburg. Quite a lot of Russians had a house, because they spent more time there, or they enjoyed the life. But we had our grandfather's flat, and the grand rooms there were taken over by the soldiers. But we had the back. And we had, curiously enough, two faithful servants, quite young girls – one was called Pasha, and the other Manya. And they stuck with us and in fact used to make friends with the soldiers, and bring us some food. I remember once Pasha brought a vast ham. Suddenly the real meat.

But my father eventually felt he hadn't a chance, that we wouldn't survive. So he put in for a leave of absence to go to England, to find out about reinforced concrete or something like that. And they said, 'Right you can go, and you can take your wife, and you can take one of your children, but the others stay.' They wanted him back; if you got out, nobody sent you back. But the real job was to get out in those days.

So both my parents, but mostly my mother, had this appalling decision. Does she stay behind with her three little daughters, aged 6, 8 and 10, or does she go off with her husband? The first thing she decided was that the children stay together. 'If I can't take all of them, I won't take any of them.' Her calculation was this; that she would go with my father and as soon as she was in England, she would move heaven and earth to get us out. She also had the advantage that she could leave me with my father's brother, who lived in this flat. He – my uncle – had married the holiday governess who had come to be companion to my aunt.

97

She was a marvellous person and stuck most loyally to my uncle and certainly looked after us.

And another person who would look after us was an elderly – well she was probably 30; at that time she seemed as old as the hills – a Latvian schoolteacher. Nobody grand, just a perfectly ordinary elementary schoolteacher. When the Revolution started all the schools closed, and she was just out on her ear, and of course she didn't have any jewels, or lace, or anything to sell, so she was simply starving and begging in the streets. My mother saw her begging once and said 'I can't offer you money, but would you like to come and look after my three little girls?' And she did come, and she saw that we washed and got to bed and got up, and ate properly – did all those sort of things. We would go to the park and she would take us out, and of course my mother and my aunt spent all their time buying and selling things in order to get some sort of food.

And so eventually, in 1922, my parents left. And the first thing they did when they got to England was to decide to go to the movies. Blow me down if they didn't go and see a very good production of *Oliver Twist* of all things when you'd left your three children to starvation. I mean when we eventually joined them my mother said it was quite extraordinary that they should fall into that. She'd thought 'Oh Dickens yes, a classic; let's go and have a look at it.' Naturally she hadn't read *Oliver Twist* or she wouldn't have gone.

What happened to you?

We stayed behind and after a year we left. Yes, it took my mother a year to get us out and even then she was jolly lucky because there were three girls, and at that time they calculated on a 'useless mouth' basis. I mean, the Bolsheviks wouldn't let the boys go; they would give visas easier for girls than for boys. Now, that year was really grim – it was absolutely horrible. All I remember is that we were always hungry, always cold and we were frightfully restricted in our lives. We were living in a constant state of fear – which was a perfectly legitimate state of fear, but it was rather frightening, because there was a lot of *pas devant les enfants* going on. So that one was always conscious of people talking, and people vanishing, and people about to vanish. It was a very unnerving atmosphere; the whole of life was twisted around in some strange way. We were walking along the Neva, and my little sister dropped her mitt, and a perfectly ordinary soldier picked it up and said 'Hi, you've lost your mitt.' And I can remember to this day, I dashed up to the youth, grabbed the mitten and dashed back again, absolutely scared stiff, as if I was supping with the devil. But it was a perfectly ordinary young man for goodness sake; there wasn't really any point. But we were all so convinced that anyone in uniform was an enemy that we behaved in a totally irrational way.

We didn't go to school; we saw no other children. We would get up and we would do our lessons with my aunt who, having been a governess, was quite good. We would write letters to our dear parents – she was a great one for that, you know 'Chère Maman, nous allons bien . . .'. We did all the sort of conventional things that one did, but on a very low key. We presumably would go out for our walk, then we would have some sort of midday meal. We spoke English, French and Russian from scratch; I mean I can't remember ever learning any of these languages. Because we had an English nurse, and then Tante Marie taught us French, and it was a rule that on Mondays, Wednesdays and Fridays we spoke French, and on Tuesdays, Thursdays and Saturdays we talked English and on Sundays we talked Russian. Of course, when we were on our own we talked Russian. But that was the form at meals, or when we spoke to aunts. I read a lot; I can remember spending an awful lot of time reading. At that time there was a post, and my mother used to send *The Schoolfriend* and other sort of schoolgirl papers in English. And I read all these splendid stories about midnight feasts and things like that in the middle of that starving country, thinking you know it was like the *Arabian Nights*. Incredible these Buntys, and Bettys – they were splendid things. It was like Angela Brazil, and it was quite extraordinary – this totally different life where nobody was hungry – oh yes there was Bessie Bunter who was always hungry, but she was the fat girl; you know you always had a fat girl and then you had the snobby girl and then other ones. It was all stereotyped, but fascinating.

Once in a while we used to go across Leningrad to visit my aunt Anna. She was my father's younger sister and my cousins were just marginally older than us – and obviously found us incredibly dull. She was very lucky, because she had a faithful chef – Lex – who stayed with her, and he'd been just a peasant boy, but she'd sent him to training school. He had been to the best cookery school in Leningrad, and so he got a job in the canteens for the soldiers. One day he came to us and he said 'Madam, I hope you don't mind, but I can't bear to see the young people so hungry – we are allowed to bring provisions for our relations, and if you didn't mind, may I say you are my cousin, or aunt, or relation?' And so he used to bring some food, and some vodka. And my cousin, who was then I think 14 or so, used to go off with this vodka under his coat to barter it for bread and things like that. It is so extraordinary how – if you were a bit older – you did the most incredible things. If anybody had suspected that this young lad was carrying vodka, they would have killed him easily, or anyway knocked him out. And Lex couldn't do that – because it would have been too dangerous. But a young lad could zoom along to wherever it was. But basically it was just the dullest time of my life, the holiday when nothing really went quite right, and being hungry as well – that is really how we lived.

Once we all had chicken-pox, or some other illness. And we somehow got into a tram, and went to the outskirts of Leningrad, across the bridge, to a place called Lesnoye[1] where there was a house in which we lived – whether we rented it or not I can't quite work out. But anyway we did live there. And that was a bit more fun, because there were children in the other houses, and we were allowed to go out of the house – we didn't go for walks, we just played in the woods. We found a dead horse in one of the rooms downstairs – I can't imagine why. But anyway, there it was. Odd memories that one has.

What did you see of the Revolution?

We certainly didn't see any violence, because as I say, we were very, very protected. The one thing that all the grown ups were absolutely clear about was that they were trying not to worry us. You took absolutely no risks. I used to see people slumped in doorways or lying on a bench – but obviously they were corpses. And if my sister said 'What's that chap doing there?' My aunt would say 'Oh, he's asleep; he's asleep; don't disturb him.' You see people really did starve; there just wasn't any food. I remember once my aunt brought some grains, and the mice had been at them. And we sat there – with this sheet spread out – removing the droppings from the grain and then washing it, cooking it, and putting it in our mouth. And it was so odd because one of the ladies who was doing it – my aunt or somebody – turned and said

'Well, I never thought that we would come to this – that we would be picking out mice droppings.' And another time we had some food which paraffin had got into. But we were so hungry that we made a porridge out of it – and you've no idea how absolutely revolting the stuff tastes. It's horrible – and I really can't bear the smell of paraffin today.

We used to be searched, to see if there were incriminating documents, or jewels or anything like that, and the soldiers arrived once before my parents left. My mother had kept this *chiffre* – which was a big diamond brooch, with the Empress's initials; part of the uniform for a lady-in-waiting. You only had it on for the great parades, and you would wear an elaborate dress, for state occasions and so on. That my mother kept; she said 'No, I have received it from the Emperor's hand – I keep it.' And of course there was the question of hiding it, and that I do remember – conversations about where best to hide it. Some people said under the cistern; others said 'No, they've rumbled that one.' But anyway, my mother had a good idea – she sewed it into a teddy bear of mine. And along came the soldiers into the nursery – and of course we'd always been told, 'Not a word to anybody, just keep quiet.' That was easy, because we were so scared. And I remember perfectly well these soldiers coming in, and my mother looking very white, and they started searching around. Then one of them picked up my teddy bear and said 'Aha, a toy. Sometimes we find other toys inside. Here, give us some scissors.' And I, forgetting that we'd been told not to speak to the soldiers, said 'No, no, no, you can't cut up my teddy bear.' And yelled most horribly. And the soldier was only about 20 – and here was this yelling little girl – and so he said 'Take it, take it.'

My father was extremely lucky to get away and not be arrested – because there were lots of people who were possibly much more liberal than my father, but who were just caught in their uniform or something. This aunt Anna – with the chef – she had married an admiral, and he was simply arrested right at the beginning; you know it was perfectly appalling what they did to the naval personnel. They used to round up naval officers and put them into leaky barges, and tow them out to sea, and just let them sink. Appalling. Well, anyway they didn't do that to him, they just simply grabbed him. One day he just didn't come back home from presumably selling the odd jewellery or silver or whatever, and my aunt discovered that he was indeed in prison. She was incredibly brave; she went to Leningrad, to the prison, and she said 'I want to see the head chief' – the chap in charge of prisoners – 'because there's been a misunderstanding; they've arrested my husband.' 'And who's your husband?' 'Admiral Nebolsin.' She was kept waiting for ages, and eventually she was let in, and she took a deep breath, and she said it was as if some sort of inspiration came to her. She just said 'Look, I know these things happen, mistakes occur, but you got it absolutely wrong. My husband's main and only concern was always the welfare of his men. He would sacrifice anything, he would sacrifice his promotion, so long as he made absolutely certain that the men under him were properly and fairly treated. And it is a great mistake that you have put him into prison, because he really doesn't deserve it.' And the chap looked up and said 'Well, is that right? Thank you for telling me. You can go.' She went, extremely thankful that she was getting out of it alive, and blow me down, a day later there was a knock at the door, and there came her husband. They had let him out. One hears such extraordinarily cruel stories, and suddenly you come across a story like that. There was some sort of humanity. But I think the Bolshevik was so impressed – she was tiny Aunt Anna but she was very determined, and of course she was young and reasonably good-looking. But she didn't thank him or anything, she just made her point. So there was an extraordinary kind of mixture of absolutely hopeless brutality, and trigger-happiness and anything you like. And then there was this perfectly reasonable, or rational attitude as well.

Getting to England was really very simple, my mother having eventually got these visas to Germany, but not to England. The splendid Latvian governess of ours helped – that was the moment when Latvia[2] was independent and they were repatriating people who had somewhere to go. So she just said she was going to Latvia, and we were her nieces, and she was taking us off – the names didn't matter much.

And so we simply got on a merchant ship taking a few passengers – and we just went to Stettin. So that we didn't actually run across rivers in white sheets over the ice or do any of those exotic things that my cousins did down in Bessarabia. We simply acquired our tickets, and luggage – which was of course searched – and we went as far as Stettin, when my mother met us on the boat, and took us to Berlin, where again we had to wait for a week in order to get permits to go to England. But that was comparatively easy, whereas my governess went off to Riga and joined her family there, and lived on to the early thirties I think. We used to correspond.

We were very happy to see our mother again. I'll never forget; it was an absolute horror for her when she saw three scarecrows. Because of course she'd spent a year in England, where children wore fairly smart children's clothes. And I remember to this day that I was wearing my cousin's jacket, far too big. You see, you couldn't get even needles or thread. You couldn't mend anything. If a button came off, a button came off, and that was that. Enormous boots I remember I had because they were terribly uncomfortable. And my sister, on the contrary, was wearing baby clothes that didn't fit – a sort of dear little ruched baby's bonnet that sat on the top of her head. And my other sister was also looking pretty grim. And my poor mother had forgotten what it was like – we thought we were fine; we were warm, that was the most important thing. So she whisked us off to Berlin. I know we went to a frightfully smart hotel, which had candelabra and velvet all over the place, and off we went to one room, and mother was horrified because we were so lousy. So my first memory was of sitting in this hotel, playing with the most marvellous doll my mother had brought. She gave my sister a fountain pen – and I can't remember what she brought my little sister, because this was the extraordinary time of the hyper-inflation, 1923 in Germany, when the mark absolutely rocketed. So you would change exactly what you needed, and you changed money two or three times a day, and then you simply went and spent it, because the next day it would be right down. We went to see some friends, and bought a large box of chocolates for them, because you know things did exist. And my mother just had to change money every six hours or so.

We were the first refugees basically since the French Revolution, so people hadn't got fed up with refugees. And especially English people were very generous. There was no open door; you could only get into England if you could get somebody or other who would vouch that they would look after you, support you, and wouldn't let you go on the rates – because there was no social security. My parents' sponsor was someone called Florrie Johnson, who really lived in a tiny little house in Peckham or something like that, and was a bank clerk. She was just jolly decent, because she certainly couldn't have supported the five of us, but I mean she just was helping out. And she told her brother and her sister that there was this Russian gentleman and his wife with children, and that was the only way they could get out. And I'm sure her brother said 'For God's sake Florrie, you can't have a family round your neck.' But anyway she did, and she was our official sponsor.

Of course my mother said we couldn't go to the council schools – dear me no! So my Mama pushed off to the local convent and said 'We are refugees, and I have three little girls, and we want them to be properly educated.' And the convent took us on free, and that happened to practically everybody. Very very few people brought money out that wasn't just a few jewels. Once we'd got to England everything became perfectly straightforward. We went to school; in actual fact we even went to boarding school at one stage. I was always two years younger than any of the other children. They pushed us on to a convent in Holyhead, North Wales – so there I was at last in a boarding school like Angela Brazil. To my surprise this didn't quite work out the way I'd read; but never mind, we didn't do badly, and we were certainly extremely well educated. And eventually I got an exhibition to Oxford. Yes it was possible – you didn't have to be a genius; you just had to be reasonably bright and you got in.

I first got married in 1933/34, and then for a second time a couple of years after the war – 1946 I reckon. I have a son by my first marriage, and then we have three children between us – two daughters and a son. Life simply took its own ordinary course. I don't know how my childhood affected me later on – my teeth went rather earlier than other people's, and I never was any good at games which I always put down to, not my innate inability, but the fact that it didn't help to be starved between the ages of 3 and 10. But I wasn't tubercular, nothing really serious. And I find it practically impossible to gauge whether this really rather horrifying life in Russia during the Revolution had any repercussions later on.

EUGENIA PEACOCK

Eugenia Peacock is the great-granddaughter of a Lancashire farmer who came to Russia looking for work and stayed. In 1918 her family was given three days to leave their estate in the Tver province.[1] They led a peripatetic existence for the next fourteen years, travelling and working in Soviet Central Asia. After her parents died, Eugenia left the Soviet Union and lived in Peking and Italy before arriving in England in 1943.

I was born in 1912 at Mashuk, an estate belonging to Mikhail Ivanovich Petrunkevich, the husband of my father's aunt Yelizaveta (aunt Liza). They had asked my father to be manager of their estate. My father's grandfather, Charles Peacock, was the son of a Lancashire farmer and his main interest was farming. When he married he was looking for a job and happened to see an advertisement saying that someone in the Tambov[2] province of Russia was looking for an estate manager. So Charles Peacock and his young wife went to Russia. They got on very well with the owner of the estate who became a great friend. I cannot remember his surname but his Christian name was Dimitri and my grandfather was called after him, Dimitri Rudolph.

Rudolph Peacock was sent to school in England. When he finished school he came back to Russia and went to Moscow University where he studied philology. He was supposed to know fifteen languages, which is probably an exaggeration. But he certainly knew several European languages and later, when he was working at the British consulate in Batum,[3] he studied several Caucasian languages. He was friendly with the mountaineers of the Causasus, and published original vocabularies of Georgian, Mingrelian, Lazian, Svanetian and Apkhazian.

Rudolph Peacock married Tatiana Bakunin and her father

105

insisted that his future son-in-law should have a steady job before he married. Rudolph found a job at an American consulate somewhere in Russia. In 1881 he was appointed vice-consul at the British consulate in Batum and was later promoted to be consul. In 1891 he was appointed consul general in Odessa. He died in 1892 and was buried in Odessa. So my grandmother Tatiana then became a widow at the age of 29 with six children, the last of whom was not yet born. She received a pension from the British government but she could not afford to send the children to school in England as her husband had wished, or even to pay Miss Cave, the English governess. Tatiana went to live at Diadino, an estate which had belonged to her father. When he died he had left it to all his children, so it did not solely belong to Tatiana, but her brothers and sisters all agreed that she and her children should live there permanently, as they used it only occasionally in the summer.

My father was the eldest of the six children. He was 12 when his father died; Miss Cave left and he went to a Russian school. Father must have been like his grandfather and namesake, Charles Peacock. He loved farming, so when he grew up all he wanted to do was to stay at Diadino and farm. Diadino was an estate of about eighty desyatinas.[4] There were fields and woods with a stream running through. There was a fairly large wooden house and another smaller house called the *fliegel* at a little distance. It was built because the family was growing and they had to have more room. At one time we lived there. There was a small copse of fir trees between the two houses and a drive leading to the main road coming from Torzhok.[5] On the other side of the road, opposite the drive, there was a *skotny dvor* (cattle yard) with stables for horses, cows and sheep. There were two larch avenues, one leading to the stream where the children were taken to splash about and learn to swim in the summer. The other avenue led to a small wooded hill known as a *gorka*. On top there was a crypt where my father's grandfather, Ilya Bakunin, and his wife were buried.

My mother was born in 1888 in Torzhok. She was called Yevgeniya Kozminykh. Her father was a doctor and her mother a nurse and later a *feldsheritsa* – something like a matron or a doctor's assistant. Mother was educated at school in Tula and then at the Higher Courses for Women[6] in Moscow. One summer mother returned from Moscow to her home at Torzhok. She had an aunt who owned a small dacha near Mashuk and mother went to stay there. From Torzhok you could only get to Mashuk by horse, so she had to look for someone who could give her a lift. She went to the stables and there she was told a man called Peacock was going to Mashuk. She found him, and he agreed to take her to Mashuk. I believe that he fell in love with her there and then. He was 30, and she was 22. They met again at Mashuk, and father offered to teach her to ride on horseback. At that time women used to ride side-saddle, but father's horse, Tishina, was not used to side-saddle, so he decided to train his horse. He used to get up very early in the morning, so that no one should see him, and put on what was called the Amazonka (a riding skirt), and rode his horse side-saddle. Well of course, his sisters saw him, laughed and teased, and the stables roared with laughter.

My parents married in 1910; the first years they spent at Mashuk. I was born in 1912. I believe mother had not quite finished her course in Moscow, so while she was expecting me she wrote her thesis, completed the course and got her diploma. I remember the house in which we lived in Mashuk, riding my tricycle through the park to see father's aunt Liza who lived in the big house. When I was about 3 years old we moved to Talozhnya where father was asked to manage another estate belonging to a relation. Mother got her first job as a teacher at the village school. We lived in a nice house belonging to the school where mother taught. It faced the village green. My first memories are from this time and I remember being lifted up and shown an owl's nest in a hollow tree; three pairs of round orange eyes were looking at me. I also remember walking in a meadow where there were lots of cowslips. Then I remember sitting on the window sill with my feet dangling outside with no shoes on, and some village children came and tickled my feet. One day there was a *yarmarka*, a fair held on the green in front of the church. It was very noisy with people shouting and laughing and I remember squealing piglets and horses neighing. It must have been a holiday because the church bells were ringing. The village had wooden houses; it was not like other Russian villages which were usually just one long street, but this one had a village green.

I cannot remember how long we lived at Talozhnya – probably one year or a little longer. The First World War must have started because father then joined the army as a volunteer in 1915. He was allowed to join the Russian army because his family was in

Russia, and as a volunteer he was even allowed to choose which front he preferred. He chose the Caucasian front where the Russians were fighting the Turks. A few months later mother took a short course in nursing and joined father in Turkey at the front. I was left with my maternal grandmother at Torzhok for the winter, but in the summer my father's mother, babushka Tatiana, invited us to Diadino, and that was heaven after a cold winter mostly indoors.

After the Revolution, in the autumn of 1917, both my parents came back to Diadino, and we all stayed there until the summer of 1918. One day I was sitting on the steps of the kitchen porch with my cousin Seriozha; he was 8 and I was 6. Suddenly we saw a group of soldiers on horseback coming up the drive. Seriozha said: 'They're coming to take away the grain.' He must have heard the grown ups talk about men coming to requisition grain. In fact they came to requisition not just the grain but the house and the land – the whole estate. There was no violence; they gave us three days to pack up what we could take with us and they camped out in front of the house in tents. They allowed each family to take one peasant cart and horse to carry themselves and their belongings as far as Torzhok. The carts and horses were then to be sent back. They weren't very large those peasant carts. There was no question of taking any furniture or anything like that, just some clothes and personal things. My parents packed what they could and my mother, father, grandmother, myself and the driver, who had to take the horse and cart back, went to Torzhok.

At Torzhok, father found a little flat and we spent a very cold and hungry winter there, but it wasn't quite as bad as the next winter. One good thing happened – mother had a lot of Russian and French books which she had had to leave at Diadino. She managed to persuade the new revolutionary authorities that, as a teacher, she needed her books for her work. So, as a member of the 'working intelligentsia', she was allowed to go back and get her books from Diadino. She also brought back my teddy bear. Father used to take clothes and watches and barter with them for food at nearby villages. The villages were not yet ruined then, and the peasants were glad to get some nice things in exchange for a little flour or potatoes. I can't remember eating any meat at all that winter.

Next spring, father went to Moscow to see if he could find work, and mother went with him. He managed to get work in some office, so at least he could get ration books for us. Grandmother and I went to Bologoye,[7] a place in the country where my mother's aunt had a house. It was just a railroad station and a few houses where we spent the summer. There was a garden and children for me to play with. I remember mother coming to see us. In the autumn grandmother and I went to Moscow; we travelled by train. But when we arrived there was no means of transport at all, no trams. I remember walking a long way from the station to Sivtsev Vrazhek Street in Moscow, to Tania's flat, who was my father's cousin. I think her flat had five or six rooms and she let us have two of them.

Everything was terribly disorganised in Moscow. Food was very scarce; they introduced rationing for bread, an eighth of a pound a day each. I don't know what it was made of but it was very black and sticky, like clay. The rationing was only for bread; all the rest you had to find for yourself. This was the winter of 1919–20. It was very cold and the central heating did not work. An iron stove was installed in one of the rooms with a chimney leading out through the *fortochka* (the small opening in a window). When the wind blew the wrong way the house would fill with smoke. The stove was in aunt Tania's room. Wood was very hard to find, and sometimes father used to bring bits of old fences or whatever he could find. Sometimes as a treat I was given a raw potato cut into slices which I toasted on the hot stove and ate. The main food was millet boiled in a lot of water – a kind of very liquid gruel. Sometimes one could get potatoes, but they were mostly black with frost-bite and didn't taste very good. We did not see any meat, milk or eggs that winter, except once. Father was walking in the street one day and saw that a dead horse was lying there with people cutting chunks of meat from it. He did the same and brought home a good slice of horse meat. It tasted heavenly; it was boiled and we had it in small slices with potatoes for several days. I remember a Christmas there when somewhere somebody found a little flour. It was rye flour, just a very little, and my old grandmother made tiny brown things that could be hung on the Christmas tree. But of course they had no sugar in them, nothing really. We ate them afterwards – oh it was marvellous – and father found a little Christmas tree which had been abandoned in some yard. I remember making toys out of matchboxes, cutting out little animals.

I went to school for the first time in Moscow, aged 7. Before that mother had taught me at home and I could read and write quite well. But having grown up in the country, I felt shy among the more sophisticated Moscow children. One day we were told that each child had to bring a log of wood to help heat the school building. So next day father gave me a log of wood and I took it to school. I did not know who to give it to. It was getting late and we all had to assemble in the hall downstairs. So I put my log in the corner near our classroom door and ran to join the others. I was then asked where my log was and I went to fetch it. But it was not where I had put it. Someone had taken it. I told the teacher what had happened but she did not believe me and punished me – I had to go out of the classroom and stand in the corridor for the rest of the hour. No one had ever accused me of lying before and I felt terribly hurt.

In March I fell ill with measles. My parents decided that the only way to survive was for all of us to leave Moscow and go to the country. Somehow father found a job at the small town and railway station of Chernorechensk. The word *cherno* means black, because there was a lot of peat in that area. Some houses had to be built for the workers of a new factory under construction. It was not far from Nizhnii Novgorod, which is now called Gorky.

We travelled by train in a goods carriage which we shared with several other people; there was a stove in the middle of the carriage so we did not suffer from cold. I believe it was one of those Stolypin[8] carriages built for peasants migrating to new lands in the east. They could take cattle with the family, all in the same carriage. Well, we had no cattle then, but there was our family and some friends and we had this large cattle truck with bunks. I used to lie on the upper bunk and look at the landscape through the small window under the ceiling. It was the same railway line that Pasternak describes in *Doctor Zhivago*, and even the same time of the year – early spring. But we did not go as far as the Urals; we stopped at Chernorechensk.

The train used to stop anywhere at a small station and stay there for a whole day sometimes. Father used to go out to the nearest village to look for food, and we were always afraid that he wouldn't come back, because nobody knew when the train would start again. This journey took us ten days, because it stopped all the time, but it was fairly comfortable. I enjoyed it very much because it was fun to look out of the window. When we arrived at Chernorechensk, father was expected there and someone had prepared a marvellous meal for us. There was soup, then veal and I was given a whole glass of milk to drink! I still remember it. We had to travel by horse several miles to the village of Rastyapino[9] where father found a flat. It was a very fertile part of Russia, a very prosperous village with large wooden houses; some of them had two storeys, not the low log cabins as in Tver province. The local people usually lived on the ground floor and often let the first floor to town people who came to spend the summer in the country.

The house where we lived had a ground floor and a first floor. We lived on the first floor, and we had four rooms and a kitchen with the Russian stove and a kitchen range, so we were all right. I was 8 when we arrived there and 10 when we left. The bank of the Oka river where the village stood was high but the opposite bank was very low and in the spring it was always flooded, so later on in the summer there was very good grass there. The village people used to go and cut the grass to make hay for their cattle. Once I went with them. We had to cross the river by boat and we stayed there all day. We found blackberries and I picked some into a basket, but I'm afraid while we were coming back I was rather hungry and ate them all. My mother said 'Oh couldn't you have brought back a few?' For me those two years at Rastyapino were very happy. I remember the flat faced the village street, and there were huge birch trees in front and I used to climb up and swing in the tree which frightened my mother.

By 1922, father felt he would be happier somewhere nearer the places he knew. He heard of a job not far from Kuvshinovo,[10] Torzhok and Diadino. It was at Mogilevka – a remote place surrounded by thick woods with bears roaming about. But it was only about twenty miles from Kuvshinovo railway station. There was a convent there, which the Soviet government had decided to turn into a state farm. The nuns used to run their own farm there; they were allowed to stay on, but it was officially treated as a state farm. They had to have a director in charge and this was the job that father was offered. At Mogilevka, there were three small houses outside the walls of the convent and we were allocated one of them. Father got on very well with Mother Superior and with the nuns who continued to work on the farm as before. Soon after we arrived, a group of children was brought to Mogilevka. There had been a famine on the Volga[11] and the children were evacuated from there. They had some teachers with them and I joined their school. Later on some local people temporarily adopted some of the children. We had one girl of my age living with us; she was called Shura. She went back to her mother when things improved at Kazan[12] where she had come from.

I enjoyed playing with Shura. The woods around were very thick and there were lots of mushrooms and berries. One day, my mother, Shura and I went for a walk in the woods, and my mother heard a bird singing. She went down a little path to follow the bird, while Shura and I went straight ahead. After a little while we heard mother calling us, so we ran back and she told us that she had seen a bear. Yes, she was walking on that very narrow path which was soft because of moss, and she looked up and suddenly saw the head of an enormous bear just walking towards her. She stood there petrified, and then she saw another bear behind the first; apparently they were mother and cub. The cubs still follow their mothers when they grow up and are quite big. So when mother saw the second bear, she turned round and ran towards us because she was afraid the bears were coming our way. Nothing happened; they didn't follow her, and she said it was so beautiful to see enormous trees and this mossy path and that enormous bear walking through, and then the second one. When we lived at Mogilevka there was a nun, Olga, who used to come and help us in the house. When we left she came with us, but her sister was still at the convent. The convent was later disbanded and the nuns were dispersed. Some of them were sent to the desert in Soviet Central Asia, and most died there. I know that Olga's sister died in the desert. That was later, after we'd left.

After a few years, father went to Moscow and met an old acquaintance of his. It was the time of NEP (New Economic Policy),[13] when some private enterprise was allowed. His friend, Lev Markovich Korotkin, suggested that they organise a timber-floating business, in the woods around Kuvshinovo. So father left Mogilevka and we all moved to Kuvshinovo, a small town with a railway station and a paper factory. There was a school where my mother taught and I attended. Then Lenin died and Stalin came to power. He stopped private enterprise and my father was accused of being a Nepman, and my mother was a Nepman's wife, therefore she was chucked out of school. At that time, when NEP was liquidated[14] and the timber business finished, I was 12. Lev Markovich suggested to my father that we all go to Tashkent[15] because he had been there before and knew it. It was a long way away; people wouldn't know my father there and couldn't accuse him of being a landowner's son or a Nepman. Those were the two things which stood in his way. The train journey took five days from Moscow to Tashkent, and I hear that now it takes only three days. I remember I found it very exciting. I took a map and wrote down the names of all the stations. We went through Samara (now called Kuybyshev), Orenburg, Aktyubinsk, and then we crossed the Urals and we were in Asia. This was the beginning of the desert which was very interesting to me. It was the first time I had been south-east. Then there was Aralsk, and here we saw the Aral sea which was very blue, an extraordinary blue, with shores of yellow sands; then Kazalinsk, Kzyl-Orda, Turkestan, Arys, Saryagach and Tashkent. The stations were full of local people – Kazakhs, Kirgiz, Uzbeks – but mostly I just remember the landscape of the desert.

We arrived there in January 1925. I was almost 13 then; my birthday was on 10 February. After the Revolution there were no hotels for Soviet people anywhere, so the only place where we could stay was some private house. A distant relation of my father's had married a geologist and they were living in Tashkent, so we descended on them and they put us up in their dining room. There we stayed for more than a month. Tashkent was wonderful because it was so warm. There was no snow, only a little frost at night; the sun was shining, yet it was January. The sky was blue, the streets were very wide and they had either two or four rows of trees growing in them. The trees were very important in the summer because they gave shade. The trees grew well because there were small ditches of running water called *aruk* along the rows of trees; without them the trees would have died because it never rains in the summer there. The food situation was easier in Tashkent; there were lots of vegetables and fruit, and from 1925 until almost 1930 life was not bad at all.

It was very difficult to find anywhere to live, because many people had the same idea as us and came to Tashkent from the north. Tashkent was known as Tashkent *gorod khlebny*, Tashkent the bread town, because life was easier there. Some homeless children travelled there on the roofs of trains or on the buffers. They arrived and lived on the streets, just sitting around a little camp fire and eating whatever they could either steal or beg from people. The geologist who we lived with knew some people involved in organising a spa or a health resort at Chimgan in the mountains, probably about sixty miles or so from Tashkent. So father got a job organising the place and building some new houses there. This was very lucky for us because in the summer we were able to spend all my school holidays at Chimgan. We lived in a *kirgiz yurt* – a kind of round tent made of felt stretched on a wooden frame.

There was some snow on the mountain called Bolshoi (big) Chimgan all summer. The valley was very fertile; there was a small river and on the slopes grew walnut trees and wild apple trees. They were not crab apples; they were edible. There were little yellow plums and lots of flowers. Chimgan means green valley. Father had a room which was his office, but he also slept there. It was near the sanatorium. But mother, a schoolfriend of mine called Galya, and myself lived in a *kirgiz yurt* a little way away from the sanatorium in a small ravine with walnut trees growing and a little spring of water. We had our meals with father. He got all our meals from the sanatorium ready cooked, and so we ate in his room. We used to walk in the mountains. Sometimes we used to hire horses from the Kirgiz and ride. It was a beautiful valley with lots of wild flowers. We used to gather the wild apples and plums and take them home. There was a little river where we bathed. Sometimes we went to a Tajik[16] village which was a few miles away and was very interesting.

The following year my father found a job as assistant director at an experimental state farm in Golodnaya Steppe.[17] It was an experimental farm because it was trying to turn this salty desert into fertile fields. We would walk in the Steppe which was really a desert. It was very flat, but on the horizon you saw mountains. They were a great distance away, and sometimes there was a caravan of camels and a sort of mirage. The camels would appear very tall and one could see a little water in the distance which didn't really exist. There were snakes, and two different kinds of lizards.

In 1927 I went to Chimgan again in the summer, but I stayed with some botanists there. They had a little camp with tents where they lived on one side of the river. I had no tent, but it never rains in the summer there, so I just slept under a walnut tree. I made myself a bed of grass and had a blanket and stayed with them. We used to get food from the sanatorium, so we took turns to bring it back to the camp. Sometimes we cooked a little on a camp fire. It was great fun because they took me with them on their expeditions looking for plants. I travelled with them quite a bit. I remember I was 15; it was 1927 and I stayed the whole summer with the botanists.

In 1928 I went on a marvellous expedition to Oburdon. Father couldn't come because he was working, but an agronomist, his wife and their daughter, my mother and myself all decided to go through the mountains in Tajikistan to Oburdon. We first went to Samarkand by train and we stayed in a *caravanserai* in Samarkand. There was a courtyard and any traveller with animals could leave their horses or donkeys or camels there, and a building right round the courtyard. That was the only approximation to a hotel in Uzbekistan. The room was empty with some carpets on the floor. You had to sleep on the floor, and you could get a meal downstairs. There was usually a *chaykhana* (tea house), a kind of wooden platform outside the building and people sat there on carpets drinking tea. The local tea is *kokchai* – green tea.

From there we went to a little town called Ura-Tyube[18] and bought four donkeys. There is a mountain range called Alai.[19] To the north of it there is the Turkestan range which has a pass called Oburdon, which is 11,000 feet high. We went over this pass walking with donkeys. The donkeys carried our tent and our luggage. My mother had a weak heart and she wasn't very fit to walk in the mountains so she sometimes rode the donkey. We had snow coming up from below us; a cloud walked up the valley up the mountainside and the wind was blowing that way so the snow came up from below. The donkeys were not very happy; they kept lying down and not wanting to go so they had to be prodded on. We went a little way down, and then we decided we were all tired and must pitch the tent and have some food. We slept the night there, on the side of this mountain pass, on a small ledge near the path. The next morning, we got up and went down into the valley to a Tajik village.

The people were very welcoming, very kind. Every village or town in that part of the country has a *mikhmankhana* – a guest house – and you could stay there without paying anything. If you wanted food, then they would cook and you paid for it. But any traveller could seek shelter there for nothing. We all slept in the same room, on the floor with carpets, and we had our own blankets. We stayed there for several days. It was in a narrow gorge and Tajik children used to play on the scree. They used to get on top of it, sit on a flat stone and slide down almost to the edge of the enormous precipice going down into the river. They would stop just at the edge and run off. The women spoke to us, because we were women, but of course we couldn't understand because we didn't speak Tajik. The friends we were with could speak Uzbek and Kirgiz, but not Tajik. They made pilaf, invited us to their orchards and offered us mulberries and apricots which were ripe then. We spent several days there, and we meant to go up the valley of the river Zeravshan[20] to a glacier, but they warned us that there was a village with lots of bandits up the valley and it wasn't advisable to go there. So we decided to leave Zeravshan.

Now the time of collectivisation[21] was approaching. It was introduced in 1929 because they decided private property was against the principles of communism and socialism. The villages were made into communal farms so that everything was shared. Well there was a lot of trouble, because of course some village people were richer than others. Those who had two or three cows were regarded as *kulaks*, rich exploiters, and were very often persecuted and deported. All the cattle were put together, all the land was put together, and they all had to work on it and have equal shares of whatever was produced. Before having their shares of course, they had to deliver a very large part of it to the state, so there was a lot of trouble as you can imagine. It's not a bad idea when it is a voluntary cooperative, when people *decide* to come together and work together, but when it's pushed on them, and some people have a little more than others, of course they resist it. It was dreadful, and even worse in places where there was a lot of land and they were a bit better off than others. Collectivisation came to Central Asia a bit later in 1930. In Tashkent we had a milkman who lived on the outskirts of the town, and he couldn't have been rich – he didn't even have a donkey. He used to come and bring milk from quite a distance, carrying it on a yoke in two pails. He brought milk and yoghurt which was from his own cow. One day he came and was in tears saying: 'This is the last time I have brought you milk because they're taking my cow away and I shan't have any more.' Somebody had told him that we were English and that there was a king in England, so in very broken Russian he asked us whether it was true. We told him that we were going to China, to join my uncle Henry, so he asked us: 'And is there a Tsar where you are going?' We disappointed him because we said 'No there is no Tsar there.' It was very sad.

116

In 1930, both my parents came to Tashkent to discuss what to do; things were getting worse. After collectivisation life was difficult; there were queues for food and people were accused of being wreckers (*vrediteli*) and of deliberately sabotaging. I was 18 then, and I remember my parents asking me if I wanted to stay or get out of the USSR. I was sure that I did not want to stay, but Soviet newspapers were full of stories about depression and unemployment in the 'capitalist world'. We did not know how much of it was true and how much was Soviet propaganda. My father had no connections in England. You see my father's father had been English, but he had died when my father was only 12. So my father had spent all his life in Russia and frankly he was rather afraid. He had forgotten most of his English; he knew nobody in England; he didn't know how he would find a job. But his brother Henry was at Harbin in Manchuria, working for a French firm which bought furs in the Far East. Father thought it might be easier to get a job at Harbin. It was decided that father would go ahead and find out if he could get work while mother and I would wait at Tashkent for a while. There was another difficulty. My grandmother (my mother's mother) was living with us, and of course she was not British and would not be allowed to leave the country. She was in her seventies and in poor health. So we could not leave her alone.

Father went to Leningrad first where he had to renew his passport. He stayed at his sister Evelyn's flat. Then he left for Harbin where he stayed with his brother Henry while trying to find a job. It was not easy and took a long time. In the meantime I went on learning English and mother found a job in Tashkent – teaching illiterate and semi-literate adults. Granny was ill all that summer and then she died. It must have been in August 1930. We buried her at the cemetery just outside Tashkent. I remember that before having permission to bury someone you had to take their ration book to the bread shop to be cancelled. Mother went to get a coffin and I was sent to the shop with the ration book. As usual, there was an enormous queue in front of the shop and the people would not let me go inside because they thought I was jumping the queue. I think I was in tears then. Somehow in the end I got through and gave up granny's ration book.

Mother and I stayed on in Tashkent for a while. I remember the Russian Easter in the spring of 1931. There was a church not far from where we lived. That was the church where grandmother used to go. Mother and I decided to go to the midnight Easter service there. There were only two churches remaining open then – this one called Sergiyevskaya church, and the one at the cemetery. When mother and I arrived at the church there was an enormous crowd standing in front – people from all over Tashkent had gathered there and could not get inside. We all stood outside and waited. Then a lorry full of young komsomols[22] arrived. They were dressed as priests, monks and nuns, and they were shouting, whistling and mocking the people who had come for the service. At midnight the church door opened and the Easter procession, *Krestny Khod*,[23] came out. The people in the crowd lit their candles and sang *Khristos Voskresy* (Christ is risen),[24] drowning all the horrible noise. The procession then went round the church and even the komsomols were impressed and shut up.

Soon my mother and I decided to leave Tashkent and go to Leningrad because we had to get my British passport there. I didn't have a proper passport then because I'd never been out of the USSR. So, after having buried my grandmother, mother and I sold some of our belongings – bits of furniture that we had, and some carpets. We took it all to the market, to Voskresenski bazaar. Then we packed up, and went to Leningrad to my aunt Evelyn's flat. We were there a long time, from September 1931 to August 1932, because it took time to get my passport. Father had to write to the consulate. I joined the Institute of Foreign Languages, and went on learning English. It was summer when we left. We had to go to Moscow first because the train left from there.

We arrived at Harbin in August or September 1932 and at first stayed at uncle Henry's flat. Father had got some minor job at the office of the British consulate and later we lived in a flat in one of the houses which belonged to the consulate. In 1933 mother and I were spending the summer at Barim, a railway station on the line between Harbin and the Soviet frontier. It was a pleasant country place. There were hills, woods, a small river and masses of wild flowers. There were deer and wild boars in the woods. We had a room in a primitive cottage which belonged to two Russian men – an uncle and nephew who knew my uncle Henry. They were hunters and sometimes sold furs to him. This isolated cottage stood in a meadow on the bank of the river Yalu. There were wild pink peonies and blue irises growing in the meadow.

Mother had a weak heart but she loved the hills. We went for a walk once and on top of a hill mother had a heart attack. I think she knew it was the end. I wanted to get some help but mother asked me not to leave her. So I sat with her for a while – I do not know how long – and she died. I ran downhill then to look for someone to help me carry her down. I saw a man cutting grass by the river. It was a Russian man from the village of Barim, and his young daughter was with him. He had a horse and cart. He helped me to carry mother downhill and took us to the hunters' cottage. I sent a telegram to father and he arrived the following day. We buried mother at the little cemetery on the hill near Barim. Mother was only 45 when she died. And I was 21; it was 1933.

I went back to Harbin and lived there with father and a cousin. I taught English at an evening school and privately. I spent two summers in Korea with a Russian family, teaching their daughter. In the autumn of 1935 my father died of cancer. He was eight years older than my mother – he was 54 – and I'm still alive strangely. I spent another winter at Harbin and summer in Korea with the same Russian family, teaching their daughter.

I was alone now. I had always wanted to see Peking. So instead of going back to Harbin in the autumn I took a train to Seoul, where I stayed a few days with a Russian couple I knew slightly. I then caught a Japanese boat going to Tientsin,[25] and from there a train to Peking. I had the addresses of several people in Peking – mostly friends of my friends and acquaintances. I also had the address of a Chinese professor whom mother and I had met on the train travelling from Moscow to Harbin. All these people helped me in various ways. I loved Peking and I probably would have spent the rest of my life there had not the Japanese arrived and spoiled it. But it is just as well I left when I did. I don't think I would have liked Mao's rule any better than the Japanese.[26]

Eugenia Peacock left Peking in 1937 for Rome, and was interned at a village in Italy until 1942, when she arrived in Britain. She worked as a Russian monitor at the BBC in Caversham for more than thirty years until she retired in 1975. She now lives near Reading.

ADA NIKOLSKAYA

Ada Nikolskaya was born in the Caucasus in 1926. Her father protested against collectivisation, was imprisoned and tortured under Stalin. Ada worked in an armaments factory from the age of 16 until she developed tuberculosis. She then worked as a cartoonist in Moscow for Mosfilm. She was interviewed in Russian.

My name is Ada Yepinondovna Dara. My maiden name was Dara. That is of Greek origin. My mother was Russian – her maiden name was Prokofiev – and her origins are from the Tretyakov family, the famous collectors. The Tretyakov Gallery is in Moscow.[1] It was a rich merchant family; they had their own house, and their own estates in the middle of Ryazan.[2]

My mother was called Yekaterina Ivanovna Prokofiev. She was studying medicine when the Japanese war[3] started, and she began work as a medical orderly. She and her brother were studying medicine together, and both joined the army. At 16 she met my father, and at 16 she married, and my father was sixteen years older than her. He was 32, and that was allowed. My father was very interesting; he was born in 1879, and he was the youngest in a family who were émigrés from Greece. My paternal grandfather was a blood prince of the Greek royal family. And his family lineage is from Greek military families, famous Greek political leaders and military leaders. I was born when my father was 47 years old, so that all the relatives from my father's side were from before the Revolution. These are pre-Revolution reminiscences so to speak. My father called me Ada in honour of his aunt, Ada Venardaki. My father was extremely handsome so they told me, because I was 10 years old when my father died in prison. He was in fact a very remarkable man, a man who never went for any compromise. Completely honest, and I believe he justified his princely blood.

And now I'm going to go back to the moment when mama and papa got married. Papa was a specialist in vine-growing, and he decided to go to the Caucasus. Mother was a student studying in Moscow; she stayed there, and used to visit him in the Caucasus. They went to Arhipo Ossipovka, a beautiful place which she chose on a very steep slope. He and my mother built their house; it was a wonderful house. On one side of the slope it was one storey, and on the other it was two floors. It was not far from Tselin. This was about 1913; they married in 1911, and my eldest sister was not yet born. She was born in 1916. For five years my mother had no children; she was studying in Moscow at the Medical Institute. You had to study for four years in these Higher Institutes for Women.

During the 1914–18 war, my mother was working in the hospital. She was very hard-working and spoke beautiful French; they used to speak French when they didn't want us to understand what they were saying. And then in 1917 the Revolution started, and there was terrible worry, and my mother was terrified they would be cut off from the Caucasus. And my father of course was of Greek origin with a Greek passport. He was never very much interested in politics; he was just a kind, interesting man, nothing else. Having studied for four years, my mother gave up the Institute, and missed the exams and went off to the Caucasus to join him. And at this time also, grandmother developed stomach cancer. My older sister Yevgenya was then 2 years old, and in 1918 granny and nanny both died and mama couldn't leave her father, husband or her little daughter in these difficult times of Revolution, particularly since they were not in the village, but away on this hill. My father was by this time working in a sanatorium as an agronomist, developing the vineyards, cultivating vines and writing up his research. At this point, they started having a lot of children. Irina was born, then Valentina, then I was born. And when I was 6 months old, my parents decided to leave Arhipo Ossipovka, abandoning the house, abandoning everything.

It was already getting dangerous; the arrests had started. It was 1926; collectivisation of a kind had started. I was born in 1926 and they went to live in Novorossiysk. We had a little flat there and I remember it very well. We lived there until 1930. And when 1930 came, my mother was working, and as she had not passed her final exams, she could not work as a general practitioner. She worked in the local hospital as a surgical sister. Papa was working, and the thirties came with all their arrests, and I remember perfectly how one day they came to search us in the night, how books fell on the floor, and how they took Papa away. He was dressed in a checked coat, and he carried a little bundle that my mother had quickly gathered together. And he was arrested. It was the gradual wiping-out of the intelligentsia and father was a highly intellectual person, high up in the intelligentsia. They were arresting all academics who were researching into agriculture and were against collectivisation. I remember how we used to go and visit him when he was in prison. We sat and talked to him through a grille, and I remember it so well how everybody was shouting through this grille, trying to talk to each other. And it was so frightening. They put in people who were pronounced enemies of the people; they put their wives in also. And I was 4 years old, my eldest sister was 14, and mother of course was frightened that if she was also arrested, we would go to a children's home. Novorossiysk is a small town; everybody knows everything about everyone else – who has been arrested, when they were arrested, for how long. And of course, mother having medical work, she immediately told her boss – Marinovsky, a wonderful surgeon – and he gave her leave as not being able to cope with work – that was a term people used – so she could leave for Moscow as quickly as possible. My mother's brother Vasily Platonovich was in Moscow. He had a son and a wife. Mother sent a telegram to him; he immediately replied 'Come at once', and we arrived to stay with uncle in Moscow. But my eldest sister stayed in Novorossiysk to sell all our things. We had the most magnificent library, and furniture, and Yevgenya, at 14 years old, was left to sell all the things, running to see her father in prison, giving him news of what was happening, trying to sell whatever she could, and send some things to Moscow, because the truth was we had taken flight from Novorossiysk.

Suddenly Yevgenya found out that father had not survived the terrible torture they had put him through. There was a building with a cellar that was awash with blood. And father could not bear the torture, and with a broken bottle he cut his veins. And Yevgenya found out about this at 14 years old, but they saved Papa and did not let him die. And he was exiled; we didn't know where to, although now I can find out from documents, but it really doesn't matter – somewhere in Siberia. He was exiled for five years. Yevgenya, having sold what she could, arrived in Moscow, and managed to start work.

Mother rented a flat, so we could leave uncle and live separately, because by that time there were four of us, and only two rooms. Uncle's wife was pretty spoilt; she was an actress, and it was difficult for mother to live depending on someone else's good will. Mother worked in two different places. In the night she was on duty in some medical centre, in a factory near the Punkt. And in the morning she ran to the hospital and we used to meet her on the way to give her something to eat, because she didn't have time to come home after the night shift. She only slept in the medical centre if there was nobody needing her attention. But of course she suffered terribly, and we were still very young; I was 6 years old, and papa was in exile. Papa used to send us five roubles at a time, anything he could earn just to help mother a little bit. Yevgenya went to work. And we three were only at school. Yevgenya was in this law office.

Five years passed. And papa returns at the end of his time in prison, but because he had been a convict, he was not allowed to live in Moscow. So we carefully concealed the fact that he was our father; when friends came to the flat, neighbours, we called him by his patronymic – uncle. And papa tried to find some work. But he couldn't find any work and he started composing children's fables. We've even got some of this poetry left, in existence, but of course nobody accepted it for publication, because when he showed his documents it was not allowed, because he'd been in exile. And then father took me and my sister Valentina, who was two years older than me, to Tula, which was about 120 kilometres from Moscow. And he went as a gardener to the Park of Rest and Culture, and we went there the three of us – to make things a little easier for my mother, because to have four to feed and look after was very difficult. This was in 1936, and I was already 10 years old. And this is when I really got to know my father, in the sense that I got to know how to behave, how to lead an orderly life, how to look after the house, and how to respect the old. My father was an ideal person, and as he was at work all day, we used to go to the park; we used to spend a lot of time with him, and it made such an impression on me that I would never be able to forget. He used to feed us, look after us, make fruit compote for us. Of course it was difficult already then for food, because the coupon system had only just finished. In the thirties, you could only buy bread with coupons in Moscow. The summer came to an end. And papa is laid off because the garden work is finished, and papa decides again to go to the Caucasus, to occupy himself again with vine-growing, and then he could earn more money to support my mother a little better in the material sense.

Not a year passed but in 1937 papa is again arrested. And he was arrested for ten years without any right to correspond; he was tried by what was called the Troika. The Troika means without a judge, without an investigation, or questioning; they condemn a man, and you have to accept this judgment. We tried in vain to find out where he'd gone, what had happened, and we were never able to find out. And only now I have been able to find out that a sentence of ten years without the right to correspond meant the firing squad, without judgment and without investigation. Then of course we knew nothing, and we always thought he was alive. And I will tell you something, when the war had finished and Stalin's epoch was over, and when they started rehabilitating, my sister said to me 'Ada, as my husband works in a military organisation, let's try and find out about what happened to father.' I wrote to the place where he had been arrested in Tibrukya. I wrote to them and they sent me a paper which said that because he had been judged without trial, he was going to be pardoned, and rehabilitated, but that they cannot give me any more information, because, according to their documents, Eponiment Pavolovich Dara is a bachelor. Papa knew that if they found out that he was married, his wife and children would also suffer. There were so many people who had been arrested; they just grabbed them, and couldn't work out who was married, and who wasn't married, and who had children, and who didn't have children – there were so many miserable children – that they believed him that he wasn't married, and shot him just like that. I had to send my papers to prove that I was his daughter, and then they sent me notification that he had died from myocardial infarc-tion in 1940. But in those days they didn't even have that kind of diagnosis, and therefore I didn't believe it. So my sister said 'Come on Ada, let's ask again for a witness to his death.' Again they wrote to me; they sent me a death certificate, and I hoped that because they didn't know that he had children, perhaps they also made a mistake about his death. My mother was still alive, but we didn't subject her to the terrible shock. We were already grown up. I was married to Shoura; I was already working in the film studio; it really didn't concern anybody, and so it was unimportant that my father was arrested. When I found out that there was this organisation Memorial,[4] I decided to join this organisation, to find out in the end where my father was, when and how he died.

I want to say that my mother destroyed everything that was connected with my father; she tried to distance herself to such an extent so that no one would ever imagine that we were from the family of Tretyakov, those rich merchants; so that nobody would know. But at the same time, when we were at school studying, if we couldn't do something in our lessons, mother would help. She knew languages; she could do mathematics; she helped with the Russian language.

When the Second World War started I was studying in the eighth grade at school, and I was 15. Mama was working in the hospital; there was bombing in Moscow, and she had to run out all the time and tend the wounded, and I began to work. And all the little children in Moscow were of course evacuated, and I went with my sister to Bashkir.[5] And she had a little baby; she was included in the evacuation with the baby, and I went, aged 15, to help. Her husband, who was a very important academic, eventually came to fetch us from there, and we moved with his Institute to Stalingrad. But after six months' time there started the most terrible bombing. The Germans were flying during the day over Stalingrad, and at night there was no blackout, and they just shot from their planes at people in the street. And when I came back from work, shooting went on of people walking in the streets, and I used to have to run along the side of the streets so that I would not get hit by these bullets. And since then, I've started to love thunderstorms, because during the thunderstorms the Germans would not fly. And in Stalingrad there were terrific thunderstorms, and I used to go outside and wish for one. And when they knew that the Germans were advancing on Stalingrad, they started to evacuate us. We were taken back to Moscow in goods van trains. We hadn't been in Moscow for nine months. My mother and sisters remained in Moscow throughout the bombing, and I went to work in this armaments factory, and this is really where my health suffered a great deal. I was 16 years old. I was working sometimes for three days without coming out of the factory; we were making armaments, some kind of mines. They never really told us what we were making. There was no heating, and my hands were covered in frost-bite, all my hands were swollen, and I had a little ring on my finger which I couldn't get off. There was no food, but for those who worked for the third day running, they would give you a little brew-up of beetroot leaves. At home, my sister had just given birth to a little boy, and she didn't work, and everyone who worked was given a food ration card. As there were very few provisions, one could give in one's card, and have a meal in the factory. But I wanted food to be in the house, to be able to buy a little bread, or meat, or herring. And when I didn't come back from work, my sister who had the little baby would run with her baby to the factory, bringing me some food or other to sustain me a little. And as I say, sometimes for three days I didn't leave the factory. I was always being sent to do work that needed a great deal of precision, in spite of my only being 16 or 17 years old. And of course that all affected my health terribly. When it was thought that the war was nearly over, they announced that the academic institutions which had been taken over as munitions factories would be allowed to return to their former function, and I made the decision then to go back and finish my schooling.

All my life I had been very good at drawing, and as I only had seven years of education, I joined a Technical Institute to learn graphic drawing. I finished this technical college, and I was a very good pupil both at school and at college, and I applied to the Polygraphic Institute, specifically for applied art. I finished with a diploma in book illustration, and that is now my trade.

One of my strongest memories is of Stalin's death[6] – it was absolutely horrific. I was already working. What will happen? That was so terrible. Which way would things change? How would we all manage to exist as we all of us perfectly understood what Stalin represented, and what he had carried out, with all his repression. People used to cover their telephones in case somebody listened into them. People used to say that walls had ears, so you were frightened to talk about anything. And therefore, when Stalin died, everyone was frightened that if you didn't cry because Stalin was dead, you might be thought not to care, that you weren't sad about his death, or you had something to do with his death. Everybody was forced to wipe their eyes and everybody was let off work, and set out for his funeral. But there was a huge crush, and huge amounts of death – people squashed to death. On the day of Stalin's funeral, Prokofiev died, and they couldn't bury the composer, because they couldn't find a coffin. All the coffins in

Moscow were sold out – there were so many suffocated and crushed to death at Stalin's funeral. There were thousands of people killed. I was there; they let us out of work specifically to go to the funeral. And I was walking in the crowd with a friend from work. And she said to me 'Do you know, this is getting very dangerous; let's leave the crowd and go back, because we won't get out of here.' And so we left, and went home, quietly, quietly, so nobody noticed us; otherwise we would have been reported at work for not going to Stalin's funeral. It was extremely frightening. Most frightening was the terrible thought of not knowing what was going to happen.

CHRONOLOGY

All dates are in New Style unless otherwise indicated.

1890	Anya Troup born; died 1989.
1896	Khodynka catastrophe following the Tsar's coronation. 1,400 people crushed to death.
1901	Tatiana Vladimirovna Toporkova born.
1902	Marie Allan born.
1903	Irina Sergevna Tidmarsh born in Moscow.
1904–5	Russo/Japanese war.
1905	22 January – Bloody Sunday, the event which precipitated the first Russian Revolution.
1905	28 October – Nicholas II signs the October Manifesto.
1905	Dorothy Russell and Ludmila Mathias born.
1906	10 March – Duma opens.
1908	Sophia Wacznadze born.
1910	Tatiana Torpokova arrives in London.
1912	Eugenia Peacock born.
1913	21 February – 300th anniversary of the Romanov dynasty.
1914	Olga Lawrence born.
1914	13/14 August – Germany declares war on Russia.
1916	30 December – murder of Rasputin.
1917	Disturbances, strikes, protests and mutiny of garrisons leading to the February (OS) Revolution.
1917	15 March – Tsar Nicholas II abdicates. Provisional Government formed. From 24 July it was led by Aleksandr Kerensky.
1917	8 November – Bolshevik coup d'état.
1918	18 July – murder of Tsar and his family at Ekaterinburg.
1918–20	Russian civil war.

1920	Dorothy Russell and Irina Sergevna Tidmarsh arrive in Britain.
1921	New Economic Policy (NEP) introduced.
1921	Sophia Wacznadze arrives in Britain by ship.
1923	Olga Lawrence and her sisters leave Russia.
1924	21 January – Lenin died. His body lay in state for five days before being put in the mausoleum on 27 January.
1926	Ada Nikolskaya born.
1929–33	Collectivisation instituted by Stalin.
1943	Eugenia Peacock arrives in England.
1953	5 March – Stalin's death. Funeral held four days later on 9 March 1953.

NOTES

Dates before February 1918 are given in New Style unless indicated otherwise (NS, OS). Old Style corresponds to the Julian
calendar which was thirteen days behind the Western (Gregorian)
calendar in the twentieth century (twelve days behind in the
nineteenth century). The Bolsheviks adopted the New Style
calendar in February 1918, and therefore the October Revolution
of 1917 took place in November according to NS, and has been
celebrated as November ever since.

ANYA TROUP

1 dacha – a Russian country house.
2 The Russo/Japanese war of 1904–5 ended in humiliating defeat for
  Russia with the fall of Port Arthur in 1905. Russia signed the Treaty of
  Portsmouth with Japan on 5 September 1905 (23 August OS),
  surrendering the southern half of Sakhalin. Japan also gained the
  Liaotung Peninsula with Port Arthur, and established its control over
  Korea.
3 Tolstoy's estate was called Yasnaya Polyana. It was in the Tula region,
  due south of Moscow. The name translates to 'bright glade'.
4 In 1897, Tolstoyism was declared a dangerous sect. In 1901, Tolstoy
  was excommunicated from the Russian Orthodox church. His followers were arrested and exiled.
5 Leonid Pasternak, the artist, the father of Boris Pasternak (1890–
  1960). Boris Pasternak was a Russian poet, famous for his novel set
  during the Revolution – *Doctor Zhivago*. It was circulated secretly as
  samisdat – forbidden literature in Russia. *Doctor Zhivago* was first
  published in English in 1958.
6 Vladimir Grigoryevich Chertkov (1853–1936). He was a long-
  standing and devoted follower of Tolstoy, the executor of his will.
7 All Russian banks were nationalised a few weeks after the Bolshevik
  takeover of November 1917 (October OS). Cash and securities –
  including jewellery – were confiscated.

NOTES
TATIANA VLADIMIROVNA TORPOKOVA

1 Nevsky Prospekt is the main street in St Petersburg, running right through the city.
2 In 1861, steam-driven armoured ships began to be constructed for the Baltic fleet, and in 1869 the first sea-going battleship in the world, the Petr Velikii, was begun. By the end of the nineteenth century, the Baltic fleet included over 250 steam-driven ships.
3 The St Catherine Institute (Ekaterinensky), was founded in St Petersburg in 1798. Subsequently other St Catherine Institutes were founded in Moscow (1802), Kharkov (1811) and elsewhere. They were élite boarding schools for the daughters of the nobility.
4 The Russo/Japanese war 1904–5.
5 The Fontanka in St Petersburg is the canal running through the city.
6 The Khan of Khiva was ruler of the tiny empire founded in the sixteenth century, whose capital was Khiva. It was annexed to the Tsarist empire in 1876. The Khanate was replaced by the Khorezm People's Soviet Republic in 1920, when the Khan was overthrown by the Bolsheviks. In 1924 it was incorporated into Uzbekistan. The Emir of Bokhara was the ruler of an ancient trading territory founded in the first century AD. In the eighteenth century, the Emir founded the Mangit dynasty, which became a Russian protectorate in 1868, and was again annexed to the empire in 1876. The Emir was overthrown in 1920 by Bolshevik troops and his territory became part of Uzbekistan in 1924.
7 Georgia lost its independence in 1923, when the former USSR was established. A Soviet regime was installed by the Red army, called the Transcaucasian Soviet Federated Socialist Republic. Georgia declared its independence on 9 April 1991.
8 Mikhail Yureyvich Lermontov (1814–41) was a famous Russian Romantic poet, author of *A Hero of Our Time*. He died in a duel at the age of 27.
9 Peterhof was built by Peter the Great in 1709 as an Imperial palace to rival Versailles, eighteen miles south-west of St Petersburg on the Gulf of Finland. It became the most lavish of the Russian royal summer palaces, with thirty-nine miles of canals that connect fountains, pavilions, small palaces and gardens. Near Peterhof (now Petrovorets), is Tsarskoe Selo (means Tsar's village, now called Pushkin), the main summer residence of the Tsar with the Catherine Palace (built by the Empress Elizabeth), and the smaller Alexander Palace in its park. The park had an artificial lake, ornamental bridges, a replica Chinese village, a fake mosque, tumbling ruins and other curiosities. It now houses the Pushkin museum and the Hermitage. The first railway in the Russian empire was built from St Petersburg to Tsarskoe Selo in 1837. Before the Revolution, the court entourage, aristocratic families and officers of the Tsar's regiment all lived in the village of Tsarskoe Selo.
10 A samovar is a big metal urn used for making tea. The water is usually heated by charcoal held in an inner container.

11 Catherine the Great (1729–96), who reigned from 1762 to 1796.
12 In fact, a core curriculum was established in Russia under Catherine the Great in a 1786 statute, intended to provide a state education that was structured and comprehensive – both secular and scientific. It was intended for city dwellers, and no attempt was made to include the peasants.
13 Bestuzhevskiye Kursy were the first Russian Higher Courses for Women – equivalent but separate from the men's universities. They were established in Moscow in 1869 and soon after also in St Petersburg, Kiev and Kazan.
14 Count Shuvalov (1827–89) was a diplomat and politician who became one of Alexander II's advisers. He was opposed to liberal reforms, including the emancipation of the serfs. He was the Russian negotiator of the Treaty of San Stefano in 1878, between Russia and Turkey.
15 The Dowager Empress was Tsar Nicholas II's mother, Marie Feodorovna, who before her marriage in 1866 to Alexander III, was Princess Dagmar of Denmark. She had been engaged to Alexander's elder brother Nicholas, heir to the throne, who died of tuberculosis in 1865. On his deathbed he bequeathed both his fiancée and the Imperial throne to Alexander.
16 *Corps des Pages* – these were young boys in the élite military training establishment in St Petersburg. They were the sons of the nobility.
17 *Pirozhki* are little pies filled with meat or cabbage.
18 The Smolnyi Institute was a finishing school for aristocratic girls set up in 1764 by Ivan Betskoi, a close associate of Catherine the Great. The Institute became Lenin's headquarters after the Bolshevik takeover until March 1918, when he moved to Moscow.
19 The Socialist Revolutionary Party was founded in Russia in 1902, and in 1917 attracted strong support from peasants due to its policy of land nationalisation. It split following the Bolshevik takeover, and the party was suppressed by force in 1918.
20 The Russian civil war, 1918–20. The White army was formed from an alliance of various anti-Bolshevik elements, notably Tsarists, Socialist Revolutionaries, Kadets (liberals) and Menshevik factions.
21 Tomas Garrigue Masaryk (1850–1937) was chief founder and first president of Czechoslovakia, 1918–25.

SOPHIA WACZNADZE

1 Donetsk is in the Ukraine, north of the Sea of Azov.
2 Aleksandr Fyodorovich Kerensky (1881–1970) was a moderate Socialist Revolutionary, who headed the Provisional Government from July to October 1917 (OS). He escaped after the Bolsheviks seized power in the October Revolution, and remained in hiding until May 1918, when he emigrated to Europe. He moved to the United States in 1940. He wrote books and lectured on his experience of the Revolution.
3 Kharkov is due north from Donetsk in the Ukraine.

4 The Bolsheviks took over in the October Revolution of 1917 (8 November 1917 NS).

5 Artemovsk is in the south-west Ukraine.

6 Russian soldiers started returning from the First World War at the end of 1916, after the Brusilov offensive. By the summer of 1918 the retreat of demoralised soldiers was in full flood.

7 Borshch – beetroot soup.

8 Felix Edmundovich Dzerzhinski (1877–1926) was the son of a Polish aristocrat. He became a Bolshevik leader and, on 20 December 1917, head of the All Russian Extraordinary Commission for Combating Counter-revolution and Sabotage – the Cheka. It was the first secret police – forerunner of the KGB – set up to rid the new Soviet state of its perceived anti-Bolshevik enemies.

9 The German Imperial army came to relieve Kharkov in the Ukraine in 1918 after the Treaty of Brest-Litovsk. This treaty had ended the war between Russia and Germany, and was engineered by the Bolsheviks, who ceded the Ukraine to the Germans. The Ukraine was occupied for only a few months, until Germany itself collapsed at the end of the First World War.

10 In Moscow, the Bolsheviks encountered far more resistance to their takeover than in St Petersburg where the coup had been virtually bloodless. Teenage boys from the military academies, universities and schools defended the Kremlin from 12 to 14 November, but were overpowered. There was fierce fighting on the streets of Moscow; cadets were killed, and eventually forced to surrender and give up their arms to the Bolsheviks.

11 General Lavr Kornilov (1870–1918) was an intelligence officer during the Russo/Japanese war and, after the February Revolution, the commandant of the Petrograd military district. He guarded the Tsar and his family while they were under arrest in Tsarskoe Selo, then resigned, and went to the war front in April 1917. He was appointed Commander in Chief of Armed Forces under Kerensky, but it ended in conflict, so Kornilov resigned and was accused of attempting the abortive military coup against the Provisional Government from 9 to 12 September 1917. He was imprisoned, but later escaped and became commander of the anti-Bolshevik White army after the October Revolution in the Don region. He was killed there in a battle at Ekaterinodar.

12 Novorossiysk is in southern Russia, near to the Crimea.

13 Batum is on the Black Sea, Georgia's western coast.

14 Sinop is on the Turkish coast of the Black Sea.

15 Trabazon is in eastern Turkey.

16 Chakva is due north up the coast from Batum.

DOROTHY RUSSELL

1 Grand Duke Dmitri Pavlovich, the Tsar's nephew, was, with prince Felix Yusupov, part of the conspiracy to murder Rasputin. The latter

was the illiterate, licentious mystic who exerted a powerful influence at court largely due to his ability to help Tsar Nicholas II's heir – Alexei – during his haemophiliac bleeding episodes. On the night of 29–30 December 1916, Rasputin was lured to Prince Yusupov's home in St Petersburg, poisoned, shot, and eventually bound and thrown into the river Neva where he died by drowning.

2 Troika – a three horse carriage.

3 The Butyrki prison, Moscow, was the chief Bolshevik, and then Soviet prison. There are frequent mentions of it in Alexander Solzhenitsyn's *Gulag Archipelago*, vol. 1.

4 The Russells left Russia on 7 March 1920. They arrived in England on 20 March 1920.

IRINA SERGEVNA TIDMARSH

1 Arbat is a major street in Moscow, part of the old district of the city.

2 *Kasha* is a buckwheat porridge.

3 A famous Russian folk song.

4 The Imperial Black Sea fleet was created in 1783 under Catherine the Great.

5 Sevastopol is at the edge of the Crimea, on the Black Sea.

6 The Tula region is due south of Moscow.

7 *Khozhdenie v. narod* means literally 'going to the people'. It was a movement started by the intelligentsia and students during the 1860s and early 1870s to go out to the rural districts. Their aim was to teach the peasants to read and write as well as enlighten them politically and prepare for a gradual 'peasant revolution' through radical propaganda. By 1875 most of the active propagandists had been arrested, and the movement gradually died out.

8 Menshevik means minority in Russian. The party was formed under Martov in 1903 and it was in dispute with Lenin and his followers of the Bolshevik faction (Bolshevik means majority). The Mensheviks were opposed to Lenin's plans for a proletariat revolution, and advocated instead a liberal, capitalist regime modelled on European social democratic states. The two factions split at the 1903 Congress in London. After the Bolshevik Revolution they tried to form a legal opposition party, but in 1922 were suppressed, and most went into exile.

9 The Prechistensky Kursy were the first evening classes for workers to be established in Russia.

10 The Novgorod region is just south of St Petersburg.

11 The Provisional Government was set up following the forced abdication of Tsar Nicholas II on 15 March 1917. Led by Aleksandr Kerensky, it attempted reform, but was unable to cope with the huge problems Russia faced, not least the collapse of army morale at the front. The Provisional Government was swept aside in November 1917 by the Bolsheviks.

12 The Bolshevik Revolution took place on 8 November 1917 (NS).

13 Gomel is in Belarus, near the Ukrainian and Russian borders.
14 Restrictions on Jewish settlement, called Pale of Settlement (*cherta osediosti*), were introduced by Catherine the Great. Jews were only allowed to settle and trade in newly annexed parts of Poland and in areas around the Black Sea. The restrictions increased during the nineteenth century, and included Moscow in 1891. In 1897 almost five million Jews lived within the Pale. During the First World War, Jews abandoned the Pale, having been driven into the interior by the Russian government during the German Galician offensive of 1916. The Pale of Settlement was formally abolished by the Provisional Government in April 1917.

LUDMILA MATHIAS

1 For Tsarskoe Selo see p. 131, note 9.
2 Ludmila's father was Leonid Borisovich Krassin (1870–1926). The son of a government official, Krassin was expelled from the St Petersburg Technological Institute in 1891. He was exiled, and worked in Siberia and the Caucasus on engineering projects. During the 1905 Revolution he was a member of the St Petersburg Soviet. In 1908 he worked abroad, for German companies, while organising the Bolshevik underground movement. He returned to political activity in 1918. He was appointed Commissar for Foreign Trade in Great Britain from 1920 to 1923. In Great Britain he signed the first Anglo-Soviet trade agreement in March 1921. In 1924 he was appointed Soviet ambassador in Paris.
3 Finland was invaded by Alexander I in 1808, and became part of Russia the following year. The Russian defeat in the Russo/Japanese was (1904–5) encouraged Finnish nationalism, and after the Russian Revolution, Finland declared its independence on 20 July 1917.
4 Siemens Schuckert was a German engineering firm. Krassin became head of the firm's Moscow branch in 1912, and director of its entire Russian division in St Petersburg in 1913.
5 Maxim Gorky (1868–1936) was a Russian writer who sided with the Bolsheviks and took part in the 1905 Revolution. He spent seven years in exile in Capri, and returned to Russia in 1913.
6 Vladimir Mayakovsky (1893–1930) was the leading Russian revolutionary poet and founder of the Russian Futurist movement in 1912. (Their manifesto was called 'A Slap in the Face of Public Taste'.) His poetry was written to be declamed in front of mass audiences. He supported the Bolsheviks after the Revolution and from 1919 to 1921 he worked in the Russian Telegraph Agency painting posters and cartoons. He wrote an elegy on the death of Lenin in 1924, and committed suicide six years later.
7 Tsar Nicholas II abdicated on 15 March 1917. He and his family were murdered at Ekaterinburg (renamed Sverdlovsk in 1924) on 17 July 1918.
8 Lenin died on 21 January 1924. His body was brought to Moscow on

23 January. He lay in state for five days and nights. On 27 January the funeral was held in Red Square, and the embalmed body placed in a specially built mausoleum.

9 The House of the Nobles was a pre-revolutionary exclusive and prestigious club for the nobility, with houses in both St Petersburg and Moscow.

10 The Moscow Narodny bank – Moscow People's bank – was formed in 1912.

11 Arcos (All Russian Cooperative Society Limited) was a joint stock trading company established in London in 1920.

12 'Red Ruth' was Mrs Ruth Cavendish-Bentinck, the wife of Frederick Cavendish-Bentinck, whose son is now the Duke of Portland.

13 The Russian embassy in Paris has now moved to Boulevard Lannes.

MARIE ALLAN

1 After Nicholas II's coronation in May 1896, there was a crowd of 500,000 at Khodynka field outside Moscow, waiting to be given souvenirs and money. The wooden platforms they were standing on collapsed, the crowd panicked, and 1,400 people are thought to have died. Nevertheless the Tsar and Tsarina still went to the Coronation Ball that evening – both events were considered a bad omen for his reign. (Another bad omen was Nicholas II's own birthday – 6 May – St Job's day according to the Orthodox Church, commemorating Job's life of trial and suffering.)

2 The music for *Eugene Onegin* is by Tchaikovsky, the libretto based on Pushkin's novel in verse.

3 Maeterlinck (1862–1949), the Belgian poet and author, won a Nobel Prize in 1911.

4 The 300th anniversary of the Romanov dynasty was celebrated on 21 February 1913.

5 Brest-Litovsk is on the border between Poland and Russia, where the treaty was signed on 21 March 1918.

6 Astrakhan is in southern Russia, north of Georgia.

7 The Grand Duke Nikolai Nikolaivich was the Tsar's uncle and commander of the armed forces from 1914 to 1915, when the Tsar took over.

8 Petrovsky Park is in Moscow. It used to be on the outskirts near to the race course.

9 The Cheka – the forerunner of the KGB – was headed by Dzerzhinski. See p. 133, note 8.

10 Haparanda is on the Swedish side of the Swedish/Finnish border, on the Gulf of Bothnia.

11 Tornio is in Finland, very close to Sweden.

12 Marie Allan means Aeroflot, the Russian airline.

13 Mark Matveevich Antokolski (1843–1902) studied at the St Petersburg Academy of the Arts and lived in Italy and France. Many of his sculptures are housed in the Tretyakov Gallery in Moscow.

OLGA LAWRENCE

1 Lesnoye is just outside Leningrad. Lesnoye means forests.
2 Latvia gained independence in January 1921.

EUGENIA PEACOCK

1 The Tver province is a region north-west of Moscow, centred around the old city of Tver, now Kalinin.
2 Tambov province is in central Russia.
3 Batum is on the Black Sea in Georgia.
4 One desyatina is approximately 2.7 acres.
5 Torzhok is north-west of Moscow.
6 For the Higher Courses for Women, see p. 132, note 13.
7 Bologoye is above Torzhok, north-west of Moscow.
8 Pyotr Arkadyevich Stolypin was Russian prime minister under Nicholas II from July 1906 until his assassination in Kiev in September 1911 by a Socialist Revolutionary. One of Imperial Russia's most outstanding statesmen, he is known for his agrarian reform.
9 Rastyapino is the old name for Dzerzhinsk until 1929; it is due east of Moscow, near Gorky.
10 Kuvshinovo is in north-west Russia, near Kalinin.
11 The 1920–1 famine in the Volga followed a severe drought.
12 Kazan is due east of Moscow, in Tatarstan.
13 The New Economic Policy was introduced by Lenin on 15 March 1921. Following War Communism, it permitted foreign investment and a degree of free trade in Russia. Lenin hoped to restore the economy and get a free flow of goods. Peasants, after paying heavy taxes, could now sell their remaining goods on the open market.
14 The New Economic Policy's gradualist reformist policies were overthrown by Stalin, who instituted the collectivisation of agriculture and mass industrialisation of Russia instead. Those who were thought to have come from the privileged or land-owning classes, or who had prospered under NEP, were persecuted once it was outlawed, and eliminated by Stalin.
15 Tashkent is the capital of Uzbekistan in Soviet Central Asia.
16 Tajikistan is the southernmost Soviet republic.
17 Golodnaya Steppe is a plain on the left bank of the Syr Darya river, with three terraces, bounded to the south by the Turkestan mountain range.
18 Ura-Tyube is on the border between Uzbekistan and Tajikistan, east of Samarkand.
19 The Alai mountain range is in Tajikistan.
20 The river Zeravshan passes through Uzbekistan into Tajikistan.
21 War Communism made compulsory the requisition of food supplies, and the New Economic Policy followed. Between 1929 and 1933, collectivisation was the policy instituted by Stalin to reduce the power of the *kulaks* – prosperous peasants. They were forced to give

up their lands, and join large collective farms, and to sell what they grew to the state at low prices. Stalin aimed to start a heavy industrialisation programme with the money collected. Those who resisted were punished harshly, and deported to prison camps. The policy of collectivisation caused a major famine in the countryside from 1932 to 1933.

22 The komsomols were members of the communist youth league for 14 to 28 year olds, organised in 1918, which by 1979 had nearly thirty-nine million members. For younger children there were the Little Octobrists and the Pioneer organisations, as preparation for komsomol and eventually Communist Party membership.

23 *Krestny Khod* is an Easter procession around the church led by the priest carrying icons and incense and followed by the congregation.

24 The response to *Khristos Voskresy* (Christ is risen) is *Voiscinu Voskresy* (Indeed he is risen).

25 Tientsin is in Hopeh, China, south-east of Peking.

26 Peking was occupied by the Japanese from 1937 to 1945. In 1949 the communists established the People's Republic of China, and Peking became its capital.

ADA NIKOLSKAYA

1 The Tretykov Gallery is one of the two major art galleries in Moscow, along with the Pushkin.

2 Ryazan is in the Tula region, south-east of Moscow.

3 The Russo/Japanese war of 1904–5.

4 Memorial is a group campaigning for the truth about those who suffered and died under Stalin. Memorial's sixteenth leader and honorary president was Andrei Sakharov, until his death in December 1989. Other well-known founder members of Memorial include the poet Yevtushenko, the historians Afanasiev and Medvedev and actor Ulyanov. On 31 October 1990, a monument was put up in Moscow by Memorial – after two years of pressure on the authorities – dedicated to the millions of KGB victims who suffered in the Gulag.

5 Bashkir is the in the far eastern provinces of Siberia.

6 Stalin (1879–1953) died on 5 March 1953; his funeral was held four days later on 9 March 1953.

INDEX